H. J. Hawhe

The Eclipse from Hotel and Homecooking

H. J. Hawhe

The Eclipse from Hotel and Homecooking

ISBN/EAN: 9783744789219

Printed in Europe, USA, Canada, Australia, Japan

Cover: Foto ©Lupo / pixelio.de

More available books at **www.hansebooks.com**

"The Eclipse,"

— FOR —

Hotel and Home Cooking.

SUITABLE FOR RICH AND POOR.

PRICE, 75 CENTS.

COLUMBUS, OHIO:
GLENN, PRINTER AND BINDER.
1875.

Remarks.

The Authoress of this book has been fifteen years or more in collecting her receipts. They are from some of the best cooks in the country, gathered from the North, South, East and West.

Many of the finest cooks prefer to use the vinegar from spiced, sweet pickles, or the spiced vinegar, instead of wine or brandy. Then you have both the flavor of the fruit and spices, and is very much richer. The syrup from canned fruit is also very nice. Therefore, these receipts are recommended for your trial.

MEASURES FOR HOUSEKEEPERS.—Wheat flour, 1 pound is 1 quart. Indian meal, 1 pound 2 ounces is 1 quart. Butter (when soft), 1 pound is 1 quart. Loaf sugar (broken), 1 pound is 1 quart. White sugar (powdered), 1 pound 1 ounce is 1 quart. Best brown sugar, 1 pound 1 ounce is 1 quart. Eggs, 10 eggs are 1 pound. Flour, 8 quarts are 1 peck; flour, 4 pecks are 1 bushel.

LIQUIDS.—Sixteen large tablespoonfuls are half a pint; 8 large tablespoonfuls are 1 gill; 4 large tablespoonfuls are half a gill; 2 gills are half a pint; 2 pints are 1 quart; 4 quarts are 1 gallon; a common sized tumbler holds half a pint; a common sized wine glass holds half a gill; 25 drops are equal to 1 teaspoonful.

Receipts.

SOUPS.

MOCK TURTLE SOUP.—The stock: 1 calf's head, 2 gallons water, 2 oz. butter, 2 onions, 2 turnips, 2 carrots, 2 pieces celery, bunch herbs, 5 lbs. of beef, 8 cloves, ¼ oz. eschalots, ¼ oz. black pepper, ¼ oz. allspice. Take a calf's head with the skin on, remove the brains, and lay them aside; wash the head in cold water, in which it may lie for an hour; then put it into a stewpan with 2 gallons of cold water, and let it boil gently for an hour, removing the scum carefully; then take it out of the broth, and let it remain to be half cold, when the meat must be cut from the bones into square pieces of about an inch; the skin, which is the prime part, should have the fat left adhering to it; the tongue must be cut up in the same way; put into a stok-pot 2 oz. of butter and 2 good-sized onions, sliced; shake them over the fire till brown; then place over them 5 lbs. of coarse, lean beef, and pour over half the broth in which the head has been boiled; let it boil till all the scum be removed, then add 2 carrots, 2 turnips, 2 heads of celery, 8 cloves, ¼ oz. of eschalots, and a small bunch of savory, thyme, majoram and basil, with 3 sprigs of fresh parsley and ¼ oz. each of allspice and whole black pepper; add the bones and trimmings of the head and the remainder of the broth, and let it all stew gently for 4 hours; then strain off. This is the stock. Turtle and mock turtle soups when served are much improved by addition of a dessert spoonful to a plate of Halford Leicestershire table sauce. Thickening: 6 oz. butter, 6 oz. flour, ¼ oz. lemon peel, ¼ oz. eschalots, ¼ oz. sage and ¼ oz. savory. Put 6 oz. of butter into a clean stew-pan, and gradually blend with it 6 oz. of flour; smooth it by adding ½ pint of the stock; in another pan put ½ pint of stock with ¼ oz each of grated lemon peel, eschalots, sage and savory; boil for half an hour, strain and rub the herbs through a tamis; then blend the liquor with the thickening and strain all into the stock; let

Cook Book. 5

it simmer over the fire for an hour, with the squares of meat added, and then make ready the seasoning, as follows: The seasoning to be added must be 2 teaspoonfuls of lemon juice, 2 of mushroom catsup and 1 of anchovy and the very thin peel of a lemon ; simmer five minutes, take out the lemon peel, then add the *quenelles*, as for turtle soup, and, if required, brain-balls and egg balls, and the soup is ready for the tureen. It ought to be reduced by the boiling to 4 or 5 quarts.

OX-TAIL SOUP.—Time, 4½ hours ; 2 ox-tails, ¼ lb. of lean ham, 1½ heads celery, 2 carrots, 2 turnips, 2 onions, a bunch of savory herbs, 5 cloves, a wine glass of catsup, with three quarts of water ; cut up 2 ox-tails, separating them at the joints ; put them into a stew-pan with about 1½ oz. butter, a head of celery, 2 onions, 2 turnips and 2 carrots cut into slices, and ¼ lb. of lean ham, cut very thin ; the pepper corns and savory herbs and about ½ pint of cold water ; stir it over a quick fire for a short time to extract the flavor of the herbs, or until the pan is covered with a glaze ; then pour in three quarts of water, skim it well, and simmer slowly for 4 hours, or until the tails are tender ; take them out, strain the soup, stir in a little flour to thicken it, and add half a head of celery (previously boiled and cut into small pieces) ; put the pieces of tail into the stew-pan with the strained soup ; boil it up for a few minutes and serve. This soup can be served clear by omitting the flour and adding to it carrots and turnips, cut into fancy shapes, with a head of celery in slices ; these may be boiled in a little of the soup, and put into the tureen before sending it to the table.

CREAM SOUP.—Take the bones of a turkey, chicken or buckle of veal and make 1 quart of broth ; take the skin from 18 tomatoes, 3 sliced onions and 2 oz. of butter ; put them in a saucepan, add 1 cup of water and salt and pepper ; let this stew until the potatoes are soft, stirring constantly ; add more water and let it boil again ; then add 1 quart of milk and let boil ; add nutmeg, chopped parsley and some sugar.

JULIENNE SOUP.—Time, 1½ hours ; ¾ lb. of carrots, turnips, celery and onions, 1 large cabbage lettuce, 2 oz. of butter, 2 lumps of sugar, 5 pints of clear soup, or medium stock ; weigh ¾ lb. of the above-named vegetables, and cut them into strips of about 1½ inches long, taking care they are all of the same size ; wash them in cold water, and drain them very dry ; then put them into a stew-pan with the butter and sugar pounded ; set it over a quick fire for a few minutes, tossing them over frequently until they are covered with a thin glaze, but on no account allow the vegetables to burn ; then add 5 pints of clear

soup, or medium stock, cut the lettuce into pieces and put it into
the soup, and let it all stew gently for an hour or more.

OYSTER SOUP.—One quart of water to 1 pint of milk, 1 heaping tablespoon of butter and salt and pepper to suit the taste;
this must come to a boil, must boil well; then drop in $\frac{1}{2}$ can of
oysters; five minutes will be sufficient to cook them; some people like them cooked in the broth of the oyster alone, with a
little seasoning.

VEGETABLE SOUP.—Have your soup bone put on early, boil
well and salt and pepper well; about twenty minutes before
ready to serve add 3 or 4 sliced potatoes, 1 cup of chopped cabbage and 1 carrot; when the soup bone is first put on add 1
tablespoonful of rice and dried beans, so that they may be well
done; then before serving make a thin thickening of milk and
flour and a well-beaten egg; drop in a handful of parsley leaves.

GREEN PEA SOUP.—Four lbs. of lean beef cut into small
pieces, $\frac{1}{2}$ peck of green peas and 1 gallon of water; first boil the
empty pod of the peas in the water for one hour and strain them
off; then add the beef and boil slowly for $1\frac{1}{2}$ hours; half an
hour before serving take out the bone and add the peas; 20 minutes later $\frac{1}{2}$ a cup of rice flour and salt and pepper to taste; after
adding the rice flour stir frequently to keep from burning.

TOMATO SOUP.—Three quarts veal broth, pepper and salt to
taste, 1 carrot, $\frac{1}{2}$ cup of rice, 2 tablespoonfuls of flour mixed
with cold water, 12 tomatoes, a little ground cloves, 1 sliced
lemon and a little sugar.

CARROT SOUP.—Two lbs. of beef, 6 quarts of cold water; add
3 or 4 spoonsful of salt, 12 carrots (cut up), 3 raw potatoes (sliced),
and 2 onions, with a few cloves put in them; let all boil 7 or 8
hours, after which mash the pieces if any, and strain through a
sieve; add some rolled cracker.

BRUNSWICK CHICKEN STEW.—Two chickens and 5 quarts of
water; boil until tender; remove all the meat from the bones,
pick it fine and put it back into the broth, after taking off all the
fat; about 2 hours before dinner add 6 potatoes, chopped fine;
after chopping them, boil separately for a few moments; draw
off the water before adding them to the soup; 1 quart of tomatoes, 1 pint of sweet corn, a little cayenne pepper, 1 tablespoonfull of Worcestershire sauce and salt to taste; add 4 hard-boiled
eggs, 2 chopped and two sliced, and sprinkle in some oyster
crackers; the corn and tomatoes should be well cooked; add
the eggs and crackers last; if the tomatoes are very sour add
a spoonful of sugar.

Cook Book. 7

MUTTON SOUP.—Cut a neck of mutton into four pieces, put it aside, take a slice of the gammon of bacon and put it in a saucepan with a quart of peas, with enough of water to boil them; let the peas boil to a pulp and strain them through a cloth; put them aside, add enough water to that in which the bacon, is to boil the mutton; slice 3 turnips, as many carrots, and boil for an hour slowly; add sweet herbs, onions, cabbage and lettuce, chopped small; stew ¼ of an hour longer, sufficient to cook the mutton; then take it out, take some fresh green peas, add them, with some chopped parsley and the peas first boiled, to the soup; put in a lump of butter rolled in flour and stew till the green peas are done.

GREEN PEA SOUP.—Take some young carrots, turnips, onions, celery and cabbage-lettuces, cut them in slices and put them into a stew-pan, with a little butter and some lean ham cut in pieces; cover them closely and let them stew for a short time; fill up with stock sufficient for the soup required and let it boil until the vegetables are quite soft, adding a few leaves of mint and the crust of a roll; pound all, and having boiled a quart of peas, as green as you can, strain them off and pound them also; mix them with the rest of the ingredients and pass through a sieve; heat it and season with salt, pepper and sugar; add a few young boiled peas and use the spinach to restore it.

ECONOMICAL SOUP.—Put into a sauce-pan one-pound pieces of stale bread, 3 large onions (sliced), a small cabbage cut fine, a carrot and turnip, and a small head of celery (or the remains of any cold vegetables), a tablespoonful of salt, a tablespoonful of pepper, a bunch of parsley, a sprig of marjoram and thyme; put these into two quarts of any weak stock (the liquor in which the mutton has been put will do), and let them boil for 2 hours; rub through a fine hair sieve, add a pint of new milk, boil up and serve at once.

ENTREES.

COD FISH CAKES.—Take cod fish, prick it to pieces; let it soak over night; in the morning, boil some potatoes, and when done, mash thoroughly; then add 1 egg, well beaten, and the picked cod fish; roll in balls, and fry in hot lard until brown.

CORN OYSTERS.—Mix 1 pint of grated green corn with 3 tablespoonfuls of milk, 1 teacup of flour and ½ teacup of melted butter, 1 egg, 1 teaspoonful of salt, ½ teaspoonful of pepper; fry in butter.

The Eclipse

OMELET.—Six eggs, beat the yolks; ½ cup of milk, 1 teaspoonful of flour; melt a piece of butter the size of an egg, mix with the flour and milk, then pour this over the yolks, adding a little salt; beat the whites of the eggs to a froth, and stir them in; fry in a well-heated spider in butter; serve while hot; lay on a heated platter.

MACCARONI.—Wash it well; put it with sufficient amount of salt, into cold water, enough to allow it much swelling; hang it over the fire till tender; pour off half the water, and add as much milk, and grate on cheese to taste; let it boil till done; the whole time occupying about 45 minutes; turn with a colander; then put it into a sauce-pan with a little butter; send to the table hot.

COLD SLAW.—Cup the cabbage either in very fine strings or chop very fine; for dressing, take 3 well beaten eggs, and 1 pint of vinegar; let them come to a boil; stir in a piece of butter the size of a walnut; 1 teaspoonful of mustard, 1 of salt, ½ of pepper, ½ of sugar and ½ of cream; pour over the cabbage while hot.

POTATO PUFF.—Take 2 cups of mashed potatoes; 1 tablespoonful of butter; mix well; then add 2 eggs, well beaten, and 1 cup of milk; bake in quick oven.—*Kate St. Clair, Columbus, O.*

DRESSING FOR COLD SLAW.—Place 1 pint of vinegar on the stove; while heating, mix and beat well the yolks of 2 eggs, 1 small tablespoonful of flour, 1 tablespoonful of sugar, 1 teaspoonful of prepared mustard, ½ teaspoonful salt; do not add this mixture to the vinegar while boiling, as it may curdle; pour over the chopped cabbage, and set it in a cool place.—*H. J. H.*

MACCARONI WITH CHEESE.—Boil maccaroni in water until soft, drain off the water, then stew it with a little butter, cream and cheese, season to the taste with salt and spices; put into a dish and place in a hot oven to brown.

BAKED TOMATO.—Take six smooth round tomatoes, not too ripe, cut a slice from the smooth end of each, and with a teaspoon carefully remove the pulp; lay each slice with the tomato it was cut from; then hash one onion and a little white cabbage; crumb in two slices of light bread; add a half cup of sweet cream, a little butter and sugar, salt and pepper to taste. Fill the tomatoes, replace the covers, butter a baking pan, lay the stem side down, and bake ½ hour. If nicely done, they are a handsome dish, and are really excellent. They should be carefully taken from the baking pan.—*Miss Longlecker, Columbus, O.*

Cook Book. 9

FRIED EGG PLANT.—Cut it in slices $1\frac{1}{2}$ inches in thickness; strew a little salt over each, and lay on a plate for 10 minutes; let the water run out; dip each slice in a well beaten egg and then in rolled cracker or bread crumbs, and fry in lard as oysters. —*C. C. B. Chicago.*

CELERY SLAW.—Take 1 bunch of celery with some of the small leaves; chop it up fine with a hash knife; put a teaspoonful of butter in a stew-pan, with a little water and a pinch of salt; put the hashed celery in; let it boil five minutes. Take 1 egg and beat it well; pour a little vinegar with the egg, and an even tablespoonful of sugar; pour over the celery.—*Mrs. Mason, Columbus, O.*

POTATO SCOLLOP. — Take 6 or 8 potatoes; pare and slice thin; put into your pan a layer of potatoes, a little salt, pepper and butter, and a small amount of flour; then add another layer of potatoes; pour on enough milk to almost cover them; then bake. Sweet potatoes may be done the same way.—*Kate St. Clair.*

OMELET.—(Splendid.)—Take 6 eggs; yolks well beaten and whites to a stiff froth; 1 cup lukewarm milk, with a tablespoonful of melted butter, a tablespoonful of flour, a little salt; mix all except the whites, which last, stir briskly, and have ready the frying pan, with a little hot lard; pour in the mixture and let it brown slowly; when the eggs are set, lap the side over, and slip on a hot plate, and serve.

GREEN CORN PATTIES.—Take 12 ears of grated or scraped corn; 3 or 4 tablespoonfuls of flour; salt and pepper to taste; 1 egg; drop in small cakes in hot butter or lard.

To BOIL ARTICHOKES.—If they are young ones have about 1 inch of stalk; put them in a strong salt water for an hour or two; then put into a pan of cold water; set them over the fire, but do not cover them up, it will take off their color; when you dish them up, put rich melted butter in small cups or pots; put them in the dish with your artichokes, and send them up.

To BOIL ASPARAGUS.—Scrape your asparagus and tie them in small bunches; boil them in a pan with salt and water; before you dish them up, toast slices of bread, and dip them in the boiling water; lay the asparagus on them; pour over them melted butter, and serve hot.

BREAD AND FLITTERS.

BROWN BREAD.—Two cups of sifted Indian meal, 1 cup of rye meal, not sifted, 1 cup of wheat flour, $\frac{2}{3}$ of a cup of molasses, $1\frac{1}{2}$ pints of sweet milk or 1 quart of sour milk, 1 teaspoonful of saleratus; if an egg is added, steam $2\frac{1}{2}$ hours and bake 1 hour; without, steam 5 and bake 1.

ANOTHER WAY.—One quart of corn meal, 1 full pint of rye meal, 1 cup of molasses, 1 quart of milk and one cup of yeast; let it raise over night, then add a teaspoonful of soda; steam $3\frac{1}{2}$ hours, then bake.

HOP YEAST.—Put 6 or 8 potatoes in 1 quart of cold water and $\frac{1}{4}$ lb. of hops in a bag; put the bag in with the potatoes to boil; when the potatoes are well done pour the water from them on 1 quart of flour; then mash the potatoes well and mix with flour; add 1 tablespoonful of salt and one cup of good yeast to raise it.

POTATO BREAD.—Time to bake, $1\frac{1}{2}$ to 2 hours; $2\frac{1}{2}$ lbs. of mealy potatoes; 7 lbs. of flour; $\frac{1}{4}$ of a pint of yeast; 2 oz. of salt; boil 2 lbs. of nice mealy potatoes till floury; rub and mash them smooth; then mix them with sufficient cold water to let them pass through a coarse sieve, and any lump that remains must be again mashed and pressed through. Mix this paste with the yeast and then add it to the flour; set it to rise, well knead it and make it into a stiff, tough dough.

RYE BREAD.—Three quarts of corn meal, scalded with $2\frac{1}{2}$ quarts of boiling water, 1 tablespoonful of salt, 1 tea cup of molasses; let it cool a few minutes and add 1 quart of rye flour and 1 quart of buttermilk, with a heaping teaspoonful of saleratus stirred into it; bake 4 or 5 hours.

CORN BREAD.—One quart of sour milk, 2 tablespoons of flour, 3 eggs, $\frac{1}{2}$ teaspoonful of salt and as much corn meal as will make a stiff batter.

HARD GINGER BREAD.—One cup of butter, 2 cups of sugar, 2 cups of flour, 1 teaspoonful of saleratus dissolved in a little sour milk, 2 eggs and ginger or nutmeg according to taste.

SOFT GINGER BREAD.—One pint of molasses, 1 tablespoonful of butter, 1 egg, 1 cup of milk, 2 tablespoonfuls of ginger, 2 tablespoonfuls of baking powder and flour enough to make a stiff batter.

Cook Book. 11

CORN BREAD.—Two tablespoonfuls of butter, ½ teacup of syrup, 2 cups of fresh meal, 1 cup of wheat flour, 1 pint sweet milk, 2 eggs, 1 teaspoon of salt and 2 of baking powder; mix well the meal, flour, powder and salt; then add the other articles.

BISCUIT.—One quart of flour, 2 heaping teaspoons of baking powder, ½ teaspoonful of salt, ¼ teaspoonful of shortening; mix with sweet milk or water; mix soft and do not knead; bake in hot oven.—*Mrs. A. J. H. Chicago.*

BUCKWHEAT CAKES.—One quart of buckwheat, 3 heaping teaspoonfuls of baking powder and a little salt; mix the batter with milk.

PAN-CAKES.—Same as buckwheat, substituting wheat flour.

GRAHAM GEMS.—Three teaspoonfuls of baking powder, 1 quart of Graham flour, thoroughly mixed while dry; mix with milk to a batter, then add one egg, well beaten; drop in muffin rings, or well heated muffin irons; bake in a quick oven.—*Mrs. Matson Hill, Chicago.*

MUFFINS.—Time, 20 to 30 minutes; 1½ oz. of yeast, a quart of warm milk, a teaspoonful of salt and some flour; add a quart of warm milk to 1½ oz. of yeast and a teaspoonful of salt; then mix it into rather a soft dough, with a sufficient quantity of flour for that purpose; cover it over with a thick cloth and set it to rise near the fire; when nicely raised divide it into as many pieces as you please and form them into a round with your hands; spread a thick layer of flour on a wooden tray, put the muffins on it and let them rise again; then bake them on a hot stove or plate until they are lightly colored, turning them once.

SALLY LUNN CAKES.—Mix 2 tablespoonfuls of light yeast into a pint of warm new milk, or cream if you wish the cakes very good; rub 4 oz. of butter into 2 pounds of flour, stew into it ½ a teaspoonful of salt, then pour in the milk gradually, beating up the batter with a wooden spoon as you proceed; add the yolks of 3 eggs, well beaten, and when smoothly mixed let it rise an hour before the fire; then fill your cake tins and bake 15 to 20 minutes in a quick oven.

WAFFLES.—One pint of milk, 1 teaspoonful of cream tartar; ½ teaspoonful of soda, a lump of butter the size of an egg, 4 eggs and flour enough to make a thick batter; fry in hot waffle irons greased with butter.

12   *The Eclipse*

EGG PUFFS.—Two cups of milk, 2 cups of flour, 2 eggs and a pinch of salt; bake in cups half an hour.

PUFFIT.—One cup of sugar, ½ cup of butter, 3 eggs, 3 pints of flour, 2½ cups of sweet milk, 3 teaspoonfuls of baking powder; bake 20 minutes in a slow oven.

YEAST FOR SALT-RISING.—One-half teaspoonful of salt, 1 teaspoonful of sugar, 1 pint warm water, flour sufficient to mix into tolerably thick batter; scrape in 1 small potato and beat well; set yeast early in the morning; 4 hours after stir in a handful of flour; if all right will rise in 2 or 3 hours, when make the same as light bread; knead well.—*Mrs. L. Bradley, New Albany, Ind.*

GRAHAM MUFFING.—One pint of milk, 2 cups of Graham flour, 1 cup of wheat flour, 1 egg, a little salt; bake in quick oven.

FRITTERS.—For plain fritters, grate the crumb of a penny loaf into a pint of milk over the fire, and stir it until it is very smooth; when cold, add the yolks of 5 eggs and 3 tablespoonfuls of sifted sugar, and season with grated nutmeg; fry in lard, and serve with pudding sauce.

APPLE FRITTERS.—Take the yolks of 6 eggs and the whites of 3; beat them well and strain them; then add a pint of milk, a little salt, ½ grated nutmeg, and a glass spiced vinegar; make this into a thick batter with fine flour; slice the apples in rounds; cut out the core; dust them with fine sugar, and let them stand for 2 hours; when ready, dip each slice in the batter, and fry in plenty of boiling lard over a quick fire; cover with sugar, and serve.

ANOTHER METHOD.—Make a batter with flour and yeast, adding 2 tablespoonfuls of oil to 1 lb. of flour; make it thick 2 hours before using it.

AND ANOTHER.—Make a batter as thick as paste of one tablespoonful of olive oil, a little salt, the yolks of 4 eggs, and a spoonful of orange flower water, with as much flour as will thicken it; beat the whites of 2 eggs stiff, and stir them in; make this an hour or two before it is used; dip the fruit in this batter, and fry until they are of a fine light yellow; lay them on a soft cloth, after frying, to drain; sprinkle with sugar, and serve hot.

SPANISH FRITTERS.—Cut the soft part of a French roll into lengths as thick as the finger, and of any shape; soak in cream, with pounded cinnamon and 1 beaten egg; when soaked, fry a nice brown, and serve with butter, and sugar-sauce.

Cook Book. 13

ITALIAN FRITTERS.—Are served at all good tables; they are made of fowl's livers, sweet breads, brains, fish, fruit, each mixed in butter, and fried in oil.

POTATO FRITTERS.—Boil 2 large potatoes, and sift them; boil 4 yolks and 3 whites of eggs, with 1 tablespoonful of cream, and a squeeze of a lemon; beat all to a batter for at least least ½ hour; put some lard in a stew-pan, and drop a spoonful of the batter at a time in it when it is hot; for sauce, take the juice of a lemon, cup of sugar, glass spiced vinegar, and dessert-spoonful of peach or almond water: warm together, and serve in a sauce-boat.

ANOTHER METHOD.—Slice potatoes thin, dip them in a batter seasoned with lemon and fry; serve with white sugar over them.

STILL ANOTHER.—Boil a pound of mealy potatoes, mash and sift them; add 2 tablespoonfuls of butter, the yolks of 2 eggs and a little pepper and salt; mix and roll into balls and fry brown. Some add a very little minced shalat.

CURD FRITTERS.—Rub a pint of dry curd in a mortar; add the yolks of 4 and the whites of 2 well-beaten eggs, 1 table-spoonful of sugar, ½ a spoonful of flour, and spice or flavor to suit the taste; drop the batter into a frying-pan with a little butter or fine lard.

KIDNEY FRITTERS.—Beat 4 eggs, add 1½ gills of cream, pepper and salt, parsley and chives cut fine, and chopped mush-rooms; to this batter add some of the kidney chopped with the fat from the loin of veal minced, and mix all well together; rub the pan well with butter and pour in the whole, stirring it while it cooks, so as to keep it from spreading too much; when done, hold it a minute or two before the fire to brown.

MUFFINS WITHOUT EGGS.—Make a sponge as for bread, only mix it with milk (skimmed will do) in the morning; the next morning put in enough saleratus to sweeten it, and bake on a griddle in greased rings. Any person in the habit of baking pan cakes or muffins will know how thick to make the batter, and in a few mornings it is learned by experience. Immediately after breakfast add milk and flour to the batter left in the dish to use the next morning, as the secret of having muffins without batter or eggs seems to be in having the batter stand 24 hours.

14 *The Eclipse*

TONGUE AND HAM TOAST.—Grate half a cold smoked tongue or ham, mix it with cream and the beaten yolks of eggs; simmer it over the fire; toast some thin slices of bread without the crust, butter them liberally, and cover with the mixture; good for breakfast or tea.

SALLY LUNN.—One quart flour, 4 eggs, ½ cup melted butter (or ¼ of lard), 1 cup warm milk, 1 cup warm water, 4 tablespoons yeast, 1 teaspoon salt, ½ teaspoon soda; beat eggs to a stiff froth, add the milk, water, butter, soda and salt; stir the flour to a smooth batter; beat the yeast in and set to rise in a buttered pudding dish to bake; eat hot.—*Mrs. Captain W. H. Bisbee.*

JOHNNY CAKE.—Two cups of corn meal, 2 cups of wheat flour, 2½ cups of milk, one cup of molasses, one teaspoonful of soda, a little salt; bake in a quick oven, and eat while hot; very nice for breakfast dish.—*M. G. Miller, Columbus, Ohio.*

MEATS AND SAUCES.

SWEETBREAD.—Lard them with salt pork, boil in water 15 minutes, then put them in cold water 10 minutes; put in dripping pans, dredge with flour, pepper, salt and a little mace; ½ pint of water; bake 20 minutes until brown.

VEAL DUCKS.—Make stuffing of bread, seasoned with salt and pepper, little onion and cloves. Take veal cutlets from the round, remove the bone, spread on the stuffing, and roll and tie. Roast them like young ducks.

ROAST BEEF.—The English rule for roasting meat is 15 minutes to the pound. Put your roast in a dripping pan, sprinkle well with flour, salt and pepper, have plenty of water around it; have the oven an even heat; one hour before done put in peeled potatoes enough for your dinners, and let them roast with the meat.

ANOTHER WAY.—If a rib roast, have the bones removed, and rolled in such a way as to leave a hole in the centre; fill this up with stuffing made of bread, and roast as above.

PICKLE FOR BEEF.—For 100 lbs. of beef, pork or ham, take 6 gallons of water, 9 lbs. of salt, (half coarse and half fine,) 3 lbs. sugar, 1 qt. molasses, 3 oz. of saltpetre; boil until the scum ceases to rise, and skim well; when cool, put on your beef; rub your beef first with fine salt.

Cook Book.   15

ROAST TURKEY OR CHICKEN.—After cleaning the fowl and stuffing it well with the dressing, place in your dripping pan flour well sprinkled with salt and pepper; have plenty of water round it while cooking; be careful to keep it basted, (that is to dip the water from around it and pour over it to keep it from crisping.) As a substitute for oysters in the dressing, cabbage may be used; cut up fine about as much cabbage as would equal one-third the amount of bread used in it, and mix thoroughly; one chopped onion may be added if desired.

SAUCE A LA MAITRE D'HOTEL.—This useful sauce is largely used for warming up many kinds of meat, fowl or fish, and thus making a handsome addition to a dinner. The foundation must be half a pint of clear stock, or gravy; put this into a sauce-pan and thicken with a ounce of butter rolled into as much flour as will form it into a smooth paste; stir it over the fire till well mixed, then add a teaspoonful of salt, a quarter as much Cayenne, a dessertspoonful of lemon juice, and as much very finely-minced parsley. Simmer for a few minutes, and before you serve, thicken with the well-beaten yolks of 3 eggs, stirred in with great care to keep from curdling.

POOR MAN'S SAUCE.—This sauce, notwithstanding its unpromising name, is excellent for roast turkey, and is popular even in France. Put a tablespoonful of finely-chopped parsley with a teaspoonful of grated horseradish, into a tureen; sprinkle these with a teaspoonful of salt, and add 2 tablespoonsful of oil, and 4 of vinegar. Mix all well together before you send it in.

ROAST HAM.—Take a fine ham, soak over night in luke-warm water, next morning skin and put into a baking pan with water as for roast beef; when nearly done, cover with brown sugar and stick with cloves; continue the basting until done; 1 pint of vinegar added to the gravy one hour before done, is an improvement. *Miss Longnecker.*

JELLIED CHICKENS.—Three chickens prepared as for fricasee; when boiled tender, take them from the broth, when cold skim off the oil, remove all the fat, skin and bones from two chickens, ½ box of Cox's Gelatine, and dissolve it in the broth; season with salt and cayenne pepper, add a piece of butter when the gelatine is dissolved and the broth boils; fill the ornamental part of the mould, let it cool, keeping the rest of the broth warm; when cold, fill the mould with alternate layers of the chicken and broth. The broth should be well boiled so that it will jelly.—*Mrs. G.*

A COMMON SAUCE FOR BOILED FISH.—Half a pint of veal gravy with 2 tablespoonsful of the water in which the fish has been boiled, a whole onion, and a tablespoonful of walnut catsup; simmer for a quarter of an hour, then strain, and thicken with an ounce of butter rolled in flour.

SANDWICH.—Yolks of three hard boiled eggs, 1 pound of butter, 2 teaspoonsful of table mustard, pepper and salt, mix all and rub to a cream; spread your bread, then lay on a slice of boiled ham or tongue, then another layer of bread.

BAKED PORK AND BEANS — 2 quarts of white dried beans, soaked in cold water over night; next morning boil until the beans crack open; of course the beans must be well washed and picked before being soaked; 2 pounds of pickled pork well washed and boiled in a separate pot for an hour; then half an hour before dinner put the beans in a pan and the meat in the centre of them, covering it over well with the beans; pour over a little of the water in which the beans have been boiled, and let it bake for half an hour; bake brown.—*Mrs. J. H. H.*

LIVER BALLS.—Boil a beef liver until well done, then hash very fine, salt, pepper, dredge with flour, beat 1 egg and add to it and fry in balls in hot lard; some add a little chopped celery or parsley; good breakfast dish.—*Mrs. Samuel Mc., Philadelphia, Penn.*

BOILED HAM—Boil 3 or 4 hours, according to size, skin it, set it in the oven for half an hour, then rub it over with an egg; also cover it well with bread crumbs, and set it back again in the oven.

To BOIL A TONGUE.—If your tongue be a dry one, steep it in water all night and boil it 3 hours; if you would have it to eat hot stick it with cloves, rub it over with the yolk of an egg and bread crumbs, baste it with butter and set it before the fire until it is light brown; when you dish it up pour over brown gravy.

VEAL LOAF.—Three lbs. veal, $\frac{1}{4}$ lb. salt pork, $\frac{1}{4}$ pt. of rolled crackers, salt and pepper, 1 tablespoonful sweet majorum chopped together; bake one hour and a quarter.

WM. G. DUNN & CO., Dealers in Dry Goods and Carpets, Nos. 25, 27 and 29 N. High Street, Columbus, O.

FISH AND SALADS.

SCOLLOPED FISH.—Four lbs. of fish, Halibut, boil the fish; when cool, prick it fine; boil one pint of milk with one sliced onion; take out the onion and add ¼ lb. of butter rubbed with 3 table-spoonsful of flour and salt; when cold put in a layer of fish and cream, alternating with bits of butter; on top put a thick layer of bread crumbs and a little butter, over which squeze the juice of one lemon; bake 15 minutes.

FRYING FISH.—Wash and wipe the soles perfectly dry, rub them over lightly with a little flour, and cover them with bread crumbs and the yolk of an egg; then place them in a pan of boiling dripping, or lard, sufficiently to completely cover them, and when done, place them on a dish before the kitchen fire. The inexperienced hand will thus be able to send them to table crisp, and of a beautiful brown color; but if the fat be insufficient, or not quite hot when the soles are put in the pan, they will be flabby and greasy. Too small a quantity of fat is the most common error.

TO BOIL TROUT.—Wash and dry your trout with a clean napkin, empty, and wipe very clean within; but wash him not, and give him three scotches to the bone on one side only. Take a clean kettle, and put in as much hard, stale beer vinegar, and a little spiced vinegar and water as will cover your fish, and throw in a good quantity of salt, the rind of a lemon, a handful of sliced horseradish, and a handsome light fagot of rosemary, thyme, and winter savory. Set the kettle on a quick fire, and let it boil up to the height before you put in your fish; and if there be many, put in one at a time, that they may not so cool the liquor as to make it fall; and while your fish is boiling, beat up the butter for your sauce with a ladleful or two of the liquor it is boiling in; and being boiled enough, pour the liquor from the fish; and being laid on a dish, pour the sauce over them, and strew horseradish and a little pounded ginger. Garnish with sliced lemon.—*I. W.*

FISH CHOWDER.—Take some fat pork, cut in slices and lay in the bottom of your pot; cut some fresh cod in slices, lay on top of the pork, then a layer of biscuit, then alternate with the pork and cod; put in 1 quart of water and let simmer until the fish is done; season with pepper and salt and such sauce as you like; make a thickenig of flour with a coffee cup of cream. Clam Chowder is made the same way; cut off the heads and leathery parts.—*Miss L. R. B.*

D. F. EDWARDS & CO., Manufacturers and Dealers in Boots and Shoes, No. 123 S. High Street, Columbus, O.

2

OYSTER TOAST.—Cut as many slices of bread as desired, toast and butter on both sides; have ready a mixture of the yolks of 4 eggs, well beaten, and mix with ½ pint of cream; put it in your sauce-pan and set it over the fire to simmer until thick, but not boil; stir it well to keep it smooth; when it just comes to a boil take it off; have your oysters broiled or fried, place them between the slices of toast and pour this mixture over them; serve hot. Tongue Toast may be made the same way; a few blades of mace boiled with the cream and eggs improves the taste.

FRIED EELS.—Eels should be boiled a few minutes before they are fried, then dip them in egg and rolled crackers or bread crumbs; fry in hot lard or butter.—*Miss L. B., New York.*

STEWED CODFISH.—Pick the codfish an hour before cooking; soak in water, changing the water several times; 20 minutes is long enough to stew it; make cream thickening; eat with mashed potatoes.

HALIBUT.—Rub the fish well with salt, put it in a kettle with enough boiling water to cover it; as soon as it boils remove it where it will only simmer; let it simmer for 1 hour; then take out the fish and draw the bones; put 1 oz. of flour in a sauce-pan, to which add by degrees 1 quart of cream or milk, mixing it smoothly; then add the juice of 1 lemon, 1 small onion chopped fine, a bunch of parsley, nutmeg, salt and pepper; put the mixture on the fire and stir until it forms a thick sauce; stir in ¼ lb. of butter, strain through a sieve, put a little sauce on the dish, then the fish; turn the remainder of the sauce over it, beat the whites of 6 eggs to a froth, spread over the whole and bake half an hour; it should be light brown when done.

LOBSTERS AND CRABS.—The lobster, which is in good season from September to June, should be bought living and plunged into boiling water in which a good proportion of salt has been mixed, which destroys life immediately; it must continue to boil, according to size, from 20 minutes to an hour; the crab should be boiled in the same manner, but little more than half the time is necessary.

To BROIL TROUT.—Choose trout of the middle size; empty, wash and wipe them; then dip them in melted butter, and broil them over a clear fire. Serve with parsley, butter, or Halford sauce.

Cook Book.

To Scallop Oysters.—Open a pint of oysters and put them with their own liquor in a stew-pan to heat for 5 minutes; then take them out and beard them, strain the liquor, add to it 3 oz. of butter, rolled in flour, and put the oysters in it for 5 minutes more; butter a scallop shell and strew it with crumbs, then put a layer of oysters and layer of crumbs, with thin slices of butter over them till the shell is filled; cover it with crumbs and slices of butter, and pour the liquor over, then brown in an oven and serve; seasoning may be added, if preferred, but most epicures like the natural taste of the oyster.

Lobster and Fish Salads.—A very nice and elegant dish may be made with all kinds of cold fish, and some kinds of shell fish; the following way of dressing is for a small lobster salad, and will do for all fish salads: Have the bowl half filled with any kind of salad herb you like; then break a lobster in two, open the tail, extract the meat in one piece, break the claws, cut the meat of both in small slices, about $\frac{1}{4}$ of an inch thick; arrange these tastefully on the salad; take out all the soft part of the belly, mix it in a basin with a teaspoonful of salt, half a one of pepper, 4 of vinegar, 4 of oil; stir it well together, and pour on the salad; then cover it with 2 hard eggs cut in slices, a few slices of cucumber, and, to vary, a few capers and some fillets of anchovy.

Lobster Salad.—A lobster, yolks of 2 eggs, a spoonful of made mustard, 3 tablespoonfuls of salad oil, a taste of vinegar, a little salt and some fresh lettuces or celery; pick all the meat out of the lobster, thoroughly beat the yolks of 2 new-laid eggs, beat in made mustard to taste, and, continuing to beat them, drop in 3 tablespoonfuls of salad oil; add whatever flavoring may be preferred, a taste of vinegar and some salt; mix in 6 tablespoonfuls of vinegar and the soft part of the lobster; moisten the remainder of the lobster with this, and lay it at the bottom of the bowl; cut up the lettuce, take care that it is well rolled over in the dressing, and put it over the lobster; mustard can be left out if it is not liked; the above quantity is given for the proportions, and can be increased according to the lobster employed.

Salad Mixture.—One boiled potato, 1 saltspoon of salt, 2 of white powdered sugar, 1 mustardspoonful of mustard, 1 tablespoonful of oil, 1 teaspoonful of Halford's sauce and some vinegar; boil a nice mealy potato and mash it very smooth; add all the other ingredients, and when the whole is well mixed eat it up.

CHICKEN SALAD.—The white meat of a chicken, the weight in celery, the yolk of 1 raw egg and 1 hard-boiled, a teaspoonful of salt, the same of pepper, $\frac{1}{2}$ teaspoonful of mustard, a tablespoonful of salad oil, 1 of white wine vinegar and 1 teaspoonful of extract of celery; take the white meat of a chicken, boiled, cut it small or mince it fine; take the same quantity, or more, of white, tender celery, cut small, and mix the celery and chicken together an hour or two before it is wanted, then add the dressing made thus: Break the yolk of a hard-boiled egg very fine with a silver fork, add to it the yolk of a raw egg and the pepper and salt, with $\frac{1}{2}$ tablespoonful of made mustard, work all smoothly together, adding gradually a tablespoonful of salad oil and the same of white wine vinegar; mix the chicken with the dressing, pile it up in the dish and spread some of the dressing over the outside; garnish with the delicate leaves of the celery, the white of the egg cut into rings, green pickles cut in slices, pickled beet root in slices and stars and placed alternately with the rings of egg and the leaves.

PICKLES.

GREEN TOMATO PICKLES.—Take the large, smooth apple tomato, cut in 2 or 3 slices, and about 1 good-sized onion to 4 tomatoes, also sliced; put in layers in a jar, with a slight sprinkling of salt between each layer; let them stand over night; in the morning remove from the brine, rinse in cold water, drain thoroughly; then pour over, to cover them, enough vinegar, which has previously boiled half an hour, with cloves and whole pepper; pieces of horse radish root will prevent scum rising on any pickles; pour the vinegar on while hot.

CHOW CHOW DRESSING.—One-half peck of green tomatoes, $\frac{1}{2}$ peck pickling beans, $\frac{1}{2}$ peck cucumbers, $\frac{1}{4}$ peck onions, $\frac{1}{2}$ peck dry green peppers, $\frac{1}{2}$ peck dry red peppers, 1 head of cauliflower, 1 gallon vinegar, 3 oz. curry powder, $\frac{1}{2}$ lb. mustard; mix powder and vinegar in cold vinegar, and stir it into hot vinegar; must not boil; pour while hot over the vegetables.

To PICKLE ONIONS.—Peel the smallest onions you can get, and put them into strong salt water for 2 or 3 days, changing the water every day; put them in jars, and pour boiling salt water over them 2 or 3 times; have some good vinegar, and boil it with ginger, white pepper and mace; when the vinegar is cold, pour off the salt water, and pour over the vinegar.

CUCUMBER PICKLE.—Keep the cucumbers in salt water or brine, as they keep better than when pickled, unless you have pure cider vinegar; if they have been in brine very long before using, let them soak in water for 1 or 2 days, changing the water 2 or 3 times; then prepare the vinegar the same as for the pepper, adding a lump of alum the size of a hickory nut; some add a few very small onions; let it come to a boil; then put in the cucumbers, and scald them (not cook them); in a day or two change the vinegar the same as the pepper pickles.

SWEET PICKLE.—For any kind of sweet pickle, I make a rich syrup of cider vinegar; spice to suit the taste; pour over the fruit after being prepared, boiling hot; let stand for 2 or 3 days; then pour off the vinegar; heat the same over, and pour on again; repeat this 2 or 3 times to prevent fermentation; in this case the same vinegar with a little more added, can be used, as there is no salt to kill the strength; peaches can be pared or not—some prefer them not, as they think the flavor is retained better; they should be well washed; small fruits should never be broken. Water mellon rind makes a very good sweet pickle.

MANGOES OF MELONS.—Take green melons and make a brine strong enough to bear up an egg; then pour it boiling hot on the melons, keeping them under the brine; let them stand 5 or 6 days, slit them down on one side, take out all the seeds, scrape them well in the inside, and wash them clean; then take cloves, nutmeg and pepper; put all these proportionately into the melons, filling them up with mustard seed; then lay them into an earthen pot, and take one part of mustard seed and two parts of vinegar, enough to cover them, pouring it on scalding hot; keep them closely covered.

CUCUMBER PICKLES.—Wash sufficient cucumbers to fill a three-gallon jar or tub; put on them a teacup of salt, and cover them with boiling water; let them stand over night; then pour off the water, and wipe them dry; put them in a brass kettle, and cover them with vinegar; add a piece of alum the size of a hickory nut; heat gently, but not boil, but keep them warm for 3 hours, then pour off the vinegar; put cucumbers in a jar or tub; take fresh vinegar, heat it boiling hot in a brass kettle, adding spice, mustard seed and pepper to suit the taste; skim, then pour it while boiling hot, on the cucumbers; let stand for 24 hours; then pour off and boil, and skim the vinegar; follow the boiling of the same vinegar for 3 successive days, then pour it on the cucumbers, and set aside ready for use; use good cider vinegar.

TOMATOES.—One peck of green tomatoes ; slice them in thin slices; sprinkle a tablespoonful of salt, and 2 of pulverized alum over them ; let them stand over night; 1 quart of vinegar put in a porcelain kettle ; put the tomatoes in and let come to a boil ; then pour over some cold vinegar ; let it stand 1 or 2 days; then pour off the first vinegar; take 3 pints of fresh vinegar, well spiced ; let it get scalding hot; add a little sugar, and pour over the tomatoes while hot.

SPICED VINEGAR, for Cakes, Pies and Puddings.—Prepare your fruit (any kind,) as you would for making jelly, only not putting quite so much sugar ; then to 1 quart of the juice put 1 pint of the best cider vinegar; add your cloves, cinnamon or whatever spices you prefer, in little thin muslin bags, so that there will be no drugs; let it boil a few minutes, then seal in cans or bottles; if you like it a little rich molasses may be added; some use the vinegar from spiced sweet pickles, when out of the spiced vinegar.

ANOTHER WAY, Chow-Chow (excellent).—One quart of green tomatoes, 1 doz. large cucumbers, $\frac{1}{2}$ head of cabbage, 8 large onions, 3 doz small onions ; cut all together ; salt, and let stand all day ; then let them drip all night ; add to this a 25c. box of mustard, not quite 1 lb. of brown sugar, 1 oz. of celery seed, $\frac{1}{2}$ lb. of white mustard seed, $2\frac{1}{2}$ tablespoonfuls of black pepper ; mix all together in 2 or 3 quarts of vinegar ; let come to a good boil ; then add $\frac{1}{2}$ pint of grated horse radish.—*Mrs. Akin, Columbus, O.*

GREEN PEPPER PICKLES.--Seed 1 peck of green peppers while dry ; then put in strong, salt brine ; let remain 2 or 3 days; take them out and let drip awhile ; then fill with chopped cabbage, highly spiced ; then bind them with thread so that the filling will not fall out ; then place in your stone jar ; take enough vinegar to cover the whole ; put in some spices ; let come to a good boil, and pour over the peppers ; let them stand for 2 or 3 days ; then make fresh vinegar in the same way, and pour on as before ; first, pour off the old.

MARMALADES AND JELLIES.

APPLE OR PEAR JAM.—Pare and quarter ripe juicy apples or pears, and boil them at a great distance from the fire till they become a jam ; have ready a rich syrup, and add in proportion 1 pint of syrup to 3 lbs. of fruit, and boil for a quarter of an hour ; turn out into pots.

ORANGE MARMALADE.—This delicious preserve, which requires the greatest care in preparation, is made chiefly of Seville oranges, and usually about February or March, when the Seville oranges are plentiful and in the best condition; pare the outer rind from 4 oranges for every dozen pulped, and cut the rind up into small chips; scoop out the pulp, free from seeds and from the white inner skin, weigh the pulp and rind together before you put them into the preserving-pan, and have ready heated equal weight of loaf sugar; let the pulp and peel boil half an hour, or till the chips are tender, then add the sugar; and let it boil 15 minutes longer; then fill the marmalade pots.

QUINCE MARMALADE.—Choose fine ripe quinces, and put them into boiling water over the fire till they are tender, then pare, quarter, and core them; put the cores and skins back into the water; boil till it is half reduced, and strain it; in the meantime, put the quinces over the fire, and let them stew gently with an equal quantity of sugar, pouring over them the strained liquor, breaking up the fruit with a wooden spatula, and stirring till the whole forms a rich marmalade; this will require 2 or 3 hours, after which the marmalade may be poured into pots.

PEAR MARMALADE.—Pare, divide, and core large pears, boil them in as much water as will cover them till they are tender, then take them out, and put into the same water the parings and cores of the pears; boil till half reduced, and strain; use the strained liquor, in making a syrup of ¾ of a lb. of sugar and a pint of water for every lb. of pears; when this syrup is boiled till it jellies on the spoon put in the pears and boil up, stirring them for a few minutes, till the marmalade is smooth and ready for the pots. Extract of cochineal imparts a beautiful red color to jellies, syrups, marmalades and any kind of confectionery that requires that tint; it keeps well and is perfectly healthful.

BLACKBERRY JAM.—As the blackberry, the most delicious of our native fruits, is to be had for the trouble of gathering in most parts of New England, blackberry jam is one of the cheapest of preserves; it is, moreover, a fruit of rare and excellent quality, and may be eaten not only with safety, but with beneficial effects by all; the berries are ripe and plentiful in September, and merely require nice picking, half the weight of any kind of sugar, and three-quarters of an hour boiling; the single objection to the jam is the quantity of seeds, but the jelly made from this fruit is perfect.

PEACH MARMALADE.—Pare, divide and stone the fruit, and boil for half an hour, stirring it continually; then add ¾ of a lb. of sugar to each lb. of the fruit, and one-fourth of the kernels blanched, and boil up for a quarter of an hour; the marmalade will then be ready for the pots.

STRAWBERRIES, preserved whole.—Take equal weights of strawberries and loaf sugar, put the sugar into a pan with merely sufficient water to dissolve it, and let it boil till the surface is covered with small bubbles; this will probably be in about 20 minutes; then put in the fruit, with 1 pint of red currant juice to each lb. of strawberries, which improves the color; allow it to boil 5 minutes, then put into small jars; it is not necessary to use more sugar for the currant juice, the strawberries being of themselves so sweet; red currants or raspberries, with the addition of white currant juice, black currant, apricot, or other jams, may be made in this way; the advantage over the old process is, that the quantity of jam is greater, the color finer, and the flavor of the fruit perfectly retained.

MARBLE JELLY.—Take any piece of orange, strawberry, and apple jelly of irregular form and size, and throw into a mould, shaking them together; then fill up the mould with silver jelly or any transparent colorless jelly, as cool as it will remain liquified; let it remain to be well mixed, and if tastefully arranged, this will be a pretty form of jelly.

QUINCE JELLY.—The quinces should not be very ripe; peel, quarter, and core them, and immediately put them over the fire with half a pint of water to each pint of fruit, and boil till tender, but not pulpy; pour out the whole, and leave the fruit in the juice for 6 hours, then run it through a jelly-bag. Put the juice over the fire in your preserving-pan for 20 minutes, that the water may evaporate; then add 1 pint of clarified syrup to each pint of juice, stir well, and simmer for 10 minutes, then pour into the jelly pots.

PINEAPPLE JELLY.—Cut a fresh pine in slices; cover them with powdered sugar, and leave them a few hours; then pour off, and strain to obtain a pint of the syrup; dissolve an ounce of isinglass in a pint of water and clarify it; pour over the syrup and simmer 5 minutes over the fire; add a glass of spiced vinegar from sweet pickles, and pour into a mould shaped like the pineapple; it will require to be very carefully turned out, and will then be very elegant.

Cook Book. 25

LEMON JELLY.—Time, altogether, 1 hour; peel of 4 lemons, juice of 6, 3 glasses of spiced vinegar, ¾ lb. of loaf sugar, 1½ oz of isinglass, pint of spring water; steep the thin peel of 4 lemons in ½ pint of boiling water until strongly flavored with the peel, or use extract of lemon; put the sugar, pounded with the isinglass, into a stew-pan, and boil it slowly for about a quarter of an hour or 20 minutes; then add the strained lemon juice and the water from the peel, or 1 teaspoonful extract lemon; add when cold; let it just boil up; skim it well; add the spiced vinegar, and strain it until quite clear.

ORANGE JELLY.—Time, until it almost candies; peel of 2 Seville, 2 Havana oranges, and 2 lemons, juice of 3 of each, ¼ lb. of loaf sugar, ¼ pint of water, 2 oz. of isinglass; grate the rinds of the Seville, Havana oranges, and lemons; squeeze the juice of 3 of each, strain it, and add the juice to the sugar and the water, and boil it until it almost candies, have ready a quart of isinglass jelly made with 2 oz. of isinglass; put to it the syrup, and boil it once up; strain off the jelly, and let it stand to settle before it is put into the mould.

GELETINE.—One box of geletine, dissolved in a pint of luke-warm water; grate the rind from 3 lemons, cut up and squeeze, putting all into the geletine; pint of crushed sugar, 3 pints of boiling water; stir 20 minutes; then pour in glasses.

PUDDINGS.

[From the New York Advocate.]

Formerly these were as essential as meat, and in some old families the pudding had the precedence, and was served before the meat; paste puddings are boiled in a cloth, and many kinds of fruit pudding; thin puddings are best boiled in a tin mold, with a pipe running up through the centre; sauces for puddings are served by themselves, and are made in various ways; butter and sugar, stirred to a cream, flavored with vanilla or lemon, is a good sauce for fruit puddings and for batter puddings; this is called cold sauce; some beat up the yolk of an egg with a teaspoonful of spiced vinegar and add to this sauce. Whenever a pudding is put to cook the water must boil and never be suffered to stop. The cloth should be dipped into hot water, floured well, and the pudding tied, allowing room to swell. Bread pudding swells more in boiling than batter, and this must be considered. Keep a kettle with water boiling while a pudding is in the pot, and, when the water wastes away, fill up with the hot water. To make a crust for a boiled fruit or meat pudding, peel, boil, and mash fine 8 mealy potatoes—I prefer sifting them; add ½ teaspoonful of salt, a great spoonful of butter, and the white of 1 egg, beaten in 2 great spoonfuls of water; mix in flour enough to roll it out; it is very tender and light; I use it for apples, whortleberries and cherries.

BEEFSTEAK PUDDING.—Take 1½ lbs. of tender steak and cut it into strips, which heat, and lay on each a bit of butter rolled in pepper and parsley and a bit of chopped onion; roll each piece up; have 2 potatoes parboiled; peel and cut them in slices, which lay in with the meat and dust a little pepper over; put these in the pudding paste, tie it in the pudding cloth and boil from 2½ to 3 hours; some add a dozen oysters and a veal kidney, or blanched sweetbreads, or the meat of young chickens parboiled, seasoned with bits of butter rolled in flour and mushrooms, a little salt and nutmeg and no pepper, reserving the water the chickens were parboiled in for a gravy, which, with the giblets, stew a while and thicken with a teaspoonful of butter rolled in flour.

MRS. HARDY'S PLUM PUDDING.—Put 1 dozen soft crackers to soak in 2 quarts of milk over night; add in the morning another quart, 2 lbs. of raisins, 2 lbs. of currants, ½ lb. of sugar, ¼ lb. of melted butter, 2 grated nutmegs and a teaspoonful of pounded cinnamon; stir in the fruit gradually and add 4 eggs; bake as long as plum cake; when done these puddings fall.

INDIAN MEAL PUDDING.—Take 1 pint of milk and ½ pint of water; mix and scald; on 6 tablespoonfuls of Indian meal turn the hot milk and water gradually; put in a bit of butter ½ the size of an egg, a little salt, 3 tablespoonfuls of sugar, two of molasses and 1 egg; beat all well together and bake 2 hours.

FAMILY RICE PUDDING.—Put into a deep pan ½ lb. of rice, washed and picked, 2 great spoonfuls of butter, 4 of sugar and 2 quarts of milk, with a little pounded cinnamon; bake in a slow oven; good hot or cold.

APPLE PUDDING.—Make a custard of 7 eggs to a quart of milk, omitting 4 whites; sweeten it and flavor with grated lemon peel; grate 4 large apples into the custard; beat the whites of 2 of the eggs to a froth with the juice of ½ lemon and 2 oz. of sugar, and when the pudding is partly baked spread this over the top.

APPLE TAPIOCA.—Peel apples enough to line the dish that the pudding is to be served in, and take out the cores; partially cook the apples so as not to break them; put them into the dish, fill the holes where the cores were with sugar, and scatter over a tumblerful of tapioca that has soaked in water a while; fill up the dish with hot water and keep it where it will be hot, but neither boil nor simmer; take the white of 1 egg, the juice of part of a lemon, and 2 tablespoonfuls of white sugar; beat them together and spread over the top of the pudding; while dinner is being eaten set the pudding in the oven to brown; serve with sauce made thus—my invention: Take a teacup of sugar and ½ teacup of water; boil a few minutes and add a great spoonful of butter; stir well; mix a teaspoonful of butter with the same quantity of flour; stir this into the sauce, lifting it from the fire while doing this; then let it boil once and stir it on to the yolk of an egg well beaten; flavor to suit with spiced vinegar from sweet pickles, orange-flower water, lemon rind, or bitter almonds; this sauce is good for batter pudding.

TORTULLIAS.—This recipe was given me for a tea dish, but it makes a nice dessert dish, and is cooked during dinner; take ½ pint of milk, ½ pint of sifted flour, 4 eggs, a little salt, and a spoonful of melted butter; beat the eggs and flour together, gradually turning on the milk and adding the salt and butter; butter 12 teacups, half fill them with this mixture and bake them 20 minutes; serve instantly and eat with my sauce.

TAPIOCA PUDDING.—Wash a tumblerful of coarse tapioca and put it to soak in 1½ pints of milk; when soft take it from the fire and put it into a dish; sitr in while warm a cupful of sugar and 2 great spoonfuls of butter beaten together, and the grated rind of ½ a lemon; when cold add 4 beaten eggs, ½ pint of milk, a wineglass of vinegar from spiced pickles and bake until putting in a spoon it comes out clean.

MIROTON OF APPLES.—Scald the apples and sift them without peeling and pile this high upon the dish in which they are to be served; boil 1 teaspoonful of grated lemon peel and 6 or 8 lumps of sugar in a teacupful of water; then add the yolks of 3 eggs and the white of 1, ½ oz. of butter and 1 spoonful of flour; mix the whole over the fire and stir it till quite smooth; pour this upon the apples, whisk the whites of the other 2 eggs to a froth, put them over just as the miroton is to be put into the oven; sift sugar over and bake in a moderate oven 10 or 15 minutes.

APPLE CHARLOTTE.—Take an oval tin mold with a cover, or a small-sized, deep earthen pudding-dish, and rub the inside with butter; from a stale loaf of bread cut a piece to fit the bottom of the mold; dip it in melted butter and lay it in the dish; line the sides with strips of bread ¼ of an inch thick; dip these in melted butter before using; cut them even at the top of the dish, and rub oll over inside the white of 1 beaten egg; let this stand; peel and core apples enough to fill the mold, which stew with sugar, cinnamon and a bit of butter; when nearly done, fill the mold, cover with bread and lay on a plate or cover, which press with a weight and bake an hour; turn out and serve; it stands upright and is excellent.

CROQUETTES OF RICE.—Put in a stew-pan ½ lb. of rice, 1½ pints of milk, ¼ lb. of butter; stir until boiling, then put over a slow fire, cover, and let simmer slowly till quite tender; mix well the yolks of 5 eggs, ¼ lb. of sugar, and a teaspoonful of extract of lemon, and add to the rice, stirring till the eggs thicken, but do not let them boil; then lay the rice out on a dish, and, when cold, form into balls, or any desired shape, not larger than a medium-sized apple; beat 3 or 4 eggs in a basin and dip the croquettes in singly, then into a dish of bread crumbs or powdered crackers, and again into the eggs and crumbs; and, lastly, put them into a wire basket and fry in very hot lard a nice, light yellow color; drain on a cloth and serve, neatly arranged on a napkin, with powdered sugar sifted over them.

MARLBOROUGH PUDDING.—This forms part of the Thanksgiving feast and is excellent. Take 1 quart of sifted apple, ¼ lb. of dry sponge cake, 4 eggs, the juice and grated rind of 1 lemon, ½ pint of cream, 2 tablespoonfuls of melted butter, sugar to suit and a little salt; mix all well together and bake in shallow plates lined with paste, laying over the tops citron cut in narrow strips.

BREAD PUDDING.—Grate 1 pint of bread crumbs, 1 pint of sweet milk, 2 eggs well beaten, sweeten to the taste, and flavor with lemon; ½ teaspoon of baking powder; bake in hot oven until brown on top; then put a layer of jelly over it; have the whites of 2 or 3 eggs well beaten, with a little sugar mixed in to sweeten; then spread over jelly and put in oven and bake until a light brown; eat with cream.—*Mrs. Rose, Philadelphia.*

COTTAGE PUDDING.—One egg, 1 cup of sugar, 1 of sweet milk, 1 teaspoonful of soda, 2 of cream of tartar, 1 pint of flour and a little salt; to be eaten with milk and sugar.

MOLLY PLEASANT'S PUDDING.—A layer of bits of butter, 1 of stewed sifted apple and 1 of sugar; repeat until the dish is filled; make a custard of 3 eggs to a pint of milk, flavored to suit, and pour over; bake in a moderate oven for ½ hour.

STEWED APPLE—(my way).—Peel and core ten apples, put them to stew with ½ gill of water, cover them when soft, turn them into a dish; sweeten with ½ teacupful of sugar and add a great spoonful of butter, the grated rind of a lemon and a gill of thick cream beaten up well; this is excellent at tea or dessert.

COLLEY PUDDING.—Three-quarters of a pound of stale bread grated, the same quantity of beef suet chopped very fine, 1 lb. of currants, ½ nutmeg, a few cloves, 2 or 3 eggs, 2 tablespoonfuls of cream or milk; mix these well together and make into a paste in the shape of eggs; fry them gently over a clear fire in ½ lb. of butter; let them be of a nice light brown color all over; you may add blanched almonds and sweetmeats; serve with sauce.

WAFER PUDDING.—One tablespoonful of flour, 2 oz. of butter, 2 eggs, 1 cup of milk, 1 lemon; beat the butter to a cream; sift the flour in gradually; pare and finely mince the rind of 1 lemon and add the egg yolks well and whites well beaten to the milk and mix thoroughly; bake in well-buttered sauces for 20 minutes and serve with sifted sugar; care must be taken that the oven is not too hot.

BLACK CURRANT PUDDING.—Stem your fruit, but you need top them; line the pudding basin with a thin light paste, strew sugar over it; then put in your black currants, add more sugar and 1 cup of cider, or an apple or two sliced thin; cover with a top crust, tie a cloth over it and boil for 2 hours; never put water with fruit puddings; use lemon juice, grape juice or cider.

ENGLISH PLUM PUDDING.—Take 1 lb. of raisins, 1 lb. of currants, 1 lb. of suet chopped fine, ¼ lb. of flour or bread finely crumbed, 3 oz. of sugar, 1½ oz. grated lemon peel, a blade of mace, ½ of a small nutmeg grated fine 1 teaspoonful ginger, 6 well-beaten eggs; work all well together, put into a cloth and tie it firmly, allowing room for the pudding to swell, and boil 2 hours; when it comes from the fire dip it into cold water for an instant only; this forms a coating next the cloth which prevents its breaking; serve with a rich sauce.—*Mrs. Healy, London, England.*

30 *The Eclipse*

QUEEN PUDDING.—Grate rind of a lemon; 6 eggs; mix 1 quart of milk with yolks well beaten, then 1 pint of bread crumbs, nearly a small teacup full of brown sugar, piece of butter the size of an egg and 10 cents worth of raisins; bake ½ hour; beat whites very stiff, add 1 cup of white sugar; squeeze in the juice of a lemon; when the pudding is done put a layer of soft jelly over it, then cover with the whites and put it back in the oven and bake it brown.—*M. H. H., Chicago.*

TAPIOCA PUDDING.—Put to 1 quart of warm milk 5 spoonfuls of tapioca; when soft add 2 spoonfuls of drawn butter, 4 beaten eggs, reserving whites for the top; sweeten to the taste.—*Mrs. Matson Hill, Chicago.*

APPLE TAPIOCA.—Soak 1 cup of tapioca in a large quart of warm water; when soft add 1 cup of sugar, 1 cup of sliced tart apples and a little salt; bake slowly for 1 hour; to be served with rich cream.—*Mrs. Matson Hill.*

MACCARONI PUDDING.—Boil 8 oz. of maccaroni in a quart of milk till quite tender; line your dish with a thick paste, put it in and add ½ pint of milk, with a little fresh butter; cover with a paste and bake about 45 minutes.

SNOW PUDDING.—Dissolve 3 tablespoonfuls of common starch in a little cold water, then add to it 1 pint of boiling water, and the whites of 3 eggs beaten to a froth; put into an earthen pudding dish; place in your steamer, and steam 10 minutes.—*Mrs. M. G. Miller.*

SAUCE FOR THE ABOVE.—Beat the yolks of the 3 eggs, add 1 cup of sugar, and 1 of milk; a lump of butter, the size of a walnut; and boil a few minutes.

ENGLISH PLUM PUDDING.—One lb. of grated bread crumbs, 1 lb. flour, 1 lb. butter, 1 lb. suet, 1 lb. sugar, 1 lb. raisins, 1 lb. citron, 1 lb. candied orange peel, 1 lb. currants, well dried; put all together, and mix well the night before the pudding is to be boiled; also put 2 tablespoonfuls of cinnamon, nutmeg and cloves; a teaspoonful of mace; 1 tablespoon of salt; 10 eggs, the yolks and whites beaten separately, with 3 pints of milk, the rind and juice of 1 lemon; boil in 2 puddings, from 7 to 8 hours incessantly.

ANOTHER WAY.—One cup of suet or pork chopped fine, 1 cup syrup, 1 cup fruit, 1 cup milk, 2 cups flour, 2 spoonfuls of cream tartar, 1 spoonful of soda; steam 3 hours; serve with liquid sauce.

ROLY POLY PUDDING.—One quart of flour in your pan, make a hole in the centre of it, sprinkle in a little salt, 2 teacups raw beef suet chopped very fine, water enough to mix it like pie crust; roll thin on your bread board; spread with preserves (tart preserves), then roll in a roll like rolled jelly cake; put it in a bag; give it room to swell; then put in a pot of boiling water, and boil for 2 hours, with the lid off; sauce of butter and sugar with. any kind of flavoring; nutmeg is very nice.—*Mrs. Miller.*

GERMAN PUFFS.—Six eggs, leaving out the whites of 3 for sauce; 5 tablespoonfuls of flour, a little nutmeg, 1 tablespoonful of melted butter and 1 pint of milk; bake in cups half full; for sauce beat the whites of 3 eggs to a froth, add loaf sugar and the juice of 2 oranges

APPLE FLOAT.—Take 1 pint of green or dried apple sauce; make smooth by passing through a sieve or colander; the whites of 3 eggs, beaten to a stiff froth; sugar and flavor to suit taste; beat well together; then send to table, and serve with rich cold cream.—*Mrs. M. G. Miller, Columbus, O.*

SAUCE (to be poured over cake.)—Here is a delicious dessert: One quart of thick cream, whip to a stiff froth; 1 oz. of gelatine, dissolved in 1 pint of water; when the milk is warm, stir in the cream, and sweeten to your taste.

COCOANUT PUDDING.—One grated cocoanut, 1 tablespoon of butter, 1 quart boiled milk, 2 slices stale bread, 3 eggs (whites only); sugar to your taste; 1 nutmeg; beat whites to a stiff froth, and stir into the milk and bread; bake a light brown in slow oven, ¾ of an hour; to be made day before eaten.

COLLEGE PUDDINGS.—Three-fourths of a lb. of stale bread, grated; the same quantity of beef suet, chopped very fine; 1 lb. of currants, ½ nutmeg, a few cloves, 2 or 3 eggs, 2 spoonfuls of cream or milk; mix these well together, and make into a paste in the shape of eggs; fry them gently over a clear fire, in ½ lb. of butter; let them be of a nice brown color all over; you may add blanched almonds and sweetmeats; serve them up with sauce.

SYLLABUB PUDDING.—Well beat 4 eggs; add to them 6 oz. of pounded and sifted loaf sugar, a glass of spiced vinegar, and sufficient flour to make it a very stiff batter; have a quart of milk, warm from the cow, poured upon it while you continue beating; and, when it is well frothed, put it into a buttered dish, place it in a quick oven, and bake it ¼ of an hour; serve immediately.

32   *The Eclipse*

PIES.

PASTRY.—To make fine paste for pies, requires care and nicety.
The flour must be well dried and sifted, and the butter and lard
used perfectly sweet. It is useless to make crust of rancid butter
or strong lard. Butter that is not good enough for the table is
unfit to cook with. It is impossible to disguise the flavor by any
seasoning, and the use of it ought never to be permitted.

PIE CRUST.—Two large cups of flour, $\frac{1}{2}$ teacup of lard, $\frac{1}{2}$ of
butter, sufficient for 2 pies; mix well the flour, butter and lard
together, before adding the water; then add cold water to wet it.

RAISED CRUST FOR MEAT PIES.—Boil water with a little fine
lard, or fresh dripping, or butter, in the proportion of 2 oz. of fat
to 1 pint of water; while hot, mix this with as much flour as you
will want, making the paste as stiff as you can, and yet smooth,
which it will become by kneading and beating with the rolling-
pin; when quite smooth, put into a cloth or under a pan until
nearly cold; this paste can be molded into any desired form,
and will retain its shape; it may be rolled out and cut to line a
tin mold; this retains its form while baking, and the pie is served
on a platter.

SQUASH PIES.—These are very delicate; choose the Winter
Crook-neck squash; cut it up, skin the outside, and take out the
inside; stew it like pumpkin; sift it, and allow to each quart of
the sifted squash 3 pints of milk, $\frac{1}{2}$ gill of molasses, a cup of white
sugar, and a little salt; if not sweet enough, add more sugar, and
6 eggs beaten and strained; bake, like pumpkin pie, in shallow
pie plates lined with paste; some recommend nutmeg and lemon
for seasoning, but the mixture is unpleasant; the flavor in sweets
of the two combined is like turpentine.

VERY LIGHT PASTE.—Mix flour and water together; roll out
the paste, and lay bits of butter upon it; beat up the white of an
egg, and brush it all over the paste; fold it up, and roll out; then
stick upon it more butter; sprinkle over the egg; fold it over and
roll out, and repeat this until the white of the egg is used up.

FOR TARTS AND CHEESE CAKES.—Sift $\frac{3}{4}$ lb. of flour; mix the
white of an egg with a gill of water, or enough to make it into
a stiff paste; roll it; then lay the third part of $\frac{1}{2}$ lb. of butter in
bits upon it; flour, and roll it up tight; repeat this until the $\frac{1}{2}$ lb.
of butter is used.

Cook Book. 33

PUFF PASTE.—Allow a lb. of sweet-salted butter to 1 lb. of flour; sift the flour, and make a hole in the center, in which put ½ pint of cold water and 2 beaten eggs; knead it into a lump of the consistency of butter, rolling it well with the right hand until it has a clear, smooth appearance; flour the board; press the paste down; form the butter into a ball; put it upon the paste, pressing it, and drawing up the edges as if making a dumpling; flour the board well and roll it out long—(this is called the first turn); fold the paste in three; flour and roll again, which will be the second; fold again in three, and put it in a cold place, upon the ice if convenient, covering it with a damp cloth until it is required for use, when it will require four more turns.

COMMON PASTE.—To a pound and a half of flour allow ¾ lb. of butter, ¼ lb. of lard, ½ teaspoonful of salt, and 1 egg beaten in nearly a pint of water; rub the lard into the flour; pour in the wetting; beat it up with a knife; flour the board; roll out upon it the paste; spread ⅓ of the butter over it; flour thickly; roll it up tight; stand it upright; beat it down with the rolling-pin, and roll slightly from you; then spread another ⅓ of the butter, and flour and proceed as directed above; and when the last butter is rolled in, put the paste away in a dish; if it freezes, it is better. There are numberless recipes for fancy pastes, but as I have not tried them, I cannot assert their value; all paste must be made in a cool place, and the less it is worked with the hand the better.

APPLE PIE.—The apples, when perfectly ripe, do not require to be cooked, but peeled, cut into quarters, and seasoned with pounded cinnamon mixed with the sugar; orange peel, cut into fine shreds, is a nice seasoning, as well as rose water, or orange-flower water; but these last named are generally used to flavor stewed apple pies and tarts.

CRANBERRY PIE.—There are various ways to make a cranberry pie; some make it open like a custard or pumpkin pie; this is good, but not so good as to cover like an apple pie; do not stew the berries, as some do before baking, but slit each berry with a knife; this will preserve the freshness of the fruit, which is quite an important thing; a cupful of berries and an equal quantity of white sugar will make a medium sized pie; those who like a sweet pie should have more sugar—also more berries, if desired; bake as usual; a little flour sifted over the fruit gives it a thicker consistence; one thing should not be forgotten, add a small teacupful of water.

3

34   *The Eclipse*

LEMON PIE.—Take 1 lemon, 1 cup of sugar, 2 eggs, ½ cup of milk or cream, ½ cup of water, ½ soft cracker, and 2 teaspoonfuls of butter; put the sugar and lemon together; separate the whites from the yolks of the eggs, and add the liquids to the yolks and the cracker; line a plate with paste; beat all well together, and, after baking put over the top the whites beaten to a froth, with sugar, and browned a few minutes.

ANOTHER LEMON PIE, very nice.—Take a coffee-cup of sugar and 1 of milk, the juice and grated rind of a lemon, a piece of butter the size of an egg, and 6 eggs; bake in a plate lined with puff paste; beat the butter and sugar together, adding the lemon juice and grated rind; mix milk with the beaten eggs; strain and pour them into the butter and sugar, and bake long enough for the eggs to be firm.

BOSTON APPLE PIE.—Line a deep pie-dish with paste, and fill it up with apples peeled and cut into quarters; sweeten with sugar and molasses, and season with pounded cloves and allspice; cover with a crust, and bake an hour and a half; when ready to eat, break in the top crust.

POT APPLE PIE, a New Bedford Tea Dish.—Put into an iron pot a heaping quart bowl of apples peeled and quartered; strew in some powdered cinnamon, or orange-peel pounded or cut fine; strew over this a gill of sugar and 1 of molasses; have ready some dough from such as has been raised for bread; roll out a piece, and cut into pieces the size of a tumbler, ½ inch thick; lay these over the top of the apple, and cook from ¾ of an hour to an hour over the fire.

ANOTHER WAY.—Prepare the apples as above, and when they begin to cook; lay over the top pieces of stale bread or whole biscuits, and when the bread is steamed, it is ready.

CREAM PIE.—One cup of sugar, 1 egg, piece of butter size of an egg, 1 teaspoon soda dissolved in a cup of sweet milk; add to this, when mixed together, 2 teaspoons cream tartar rubbed in 3 cups of flour, and bake in 3 jelly cake tins. The cream for the inside of the pie is made as follows: One and one-half cups of milk, when boiling add 7 teaspoons corn-starch wet with cold milk; let it scald a moment, then add 2 well-beaten eggs; sweeten to taste, and flavor with lemon or vanilla. Split the cakes when cold, spread them with the cream, and put together again like jelly cake.

BOYD & ERB, Dispensing Chemists, City Hall Drug Store, No. 25 East State Street, Columbus, O.

Cook Book. 35

MINCE PIES.—There are numerous modes of making mince pies, and they are in high esteem; some use boiled tongue, some beef's heart well boiled, but the majority a piece of lean beef; venison is best: the rule is, ⅓ chopped meat, ⅓ boiled suet, and ⅓ chopped apples, adding raisins, spice and seasoning to suit, sweetening partly with molasses, and thinning with good cider.

ANOTHER RULE.—Here is a rule from a cousin whose mother's mince pies had great celebrity; to 10 lbs. of beef and 6 lbs. of suet, after boiling, add an equal weight of raisins and currants, 1 pint of molasses, the remainder of the sweetening in sugar, vinegar from spiced pickles, and cider enough to moisten the meat; spice to suit the taste, generally a little of all kinds; pack the meat and seasoning in a jar, and, when ready to bake, add to the quantity you measure out an equal measure of chopped apples, and citron to suit.

MY WAY.—For a piece of lean beef weighing 4 lbs. into a tightly covered vessel, with a gill of water, a teaspoonful of salt, and ½ salt-spoonful of cayenne; set the vessel in a stove-oven for 3 hours, and leave the meat in the dish to cool; when cold, chop it fine; to the same measure of meat, add as much and half as much more chopped apple; moisten with the juice that came from the meat in cooking; have the same measure of raisins as apples, and half the quantity of currants; stone the raisins, and put them to soften into a quart of cider; let them simmer covered; put a lb. of butter into a pint and a half of molasses; let it boil 15 minutes; then put it into the meat and stir it well; put in the raisins and cider, and season with a dozen pounded allspice, 2 dozen cloves, 2 blades of mace, a great spoonful of pounded cinnamon, ½ pint of vinegar from spiced sweet pickles; add sugar to suit, bake in covered pie dishes, and tuck in the edge to keep the juice from running out; do not make holes in the top crust of a pie; the steam escapes, and the pie is made dry thereby.

GREEN GRAPE TART.—Take the grapes when they are no larger than sweet pea seed, and clarify some sugar; throw in the grapes, simmer them for about 5 minutes; put a rim of rich crust around your dish; lay in your fruit and syrup; cover with top crust, and bake for 40 minutes; serve with custard.

CUSTARD PIE.—One quart of sweet milk, 1 cup white sugar, and 3 well-beaten eggs; flavor to suit the taste; line the pie-pans with crust; place them in the stove; then fill with the custard; bake in a hot oven until light brown.

PUMPKIN PIES.—There are pumpkin pies and squash pies; the former is the famous Thanksgiving regalement; for pumpkin pie made after the ancient mode, cinnamon and ginger were the only flavors, and most of the sweetening was molasses; but the richest of milk was used—often more than half pure thick cream—and the secret of their goodness lay in this; for cream imparts to all kinds of cookery a flavor that is inimitable. Cut up and peel a sweet yellow pumpkin; scrape out the inside, and put to stew with only the water that clings to it in washing; cover the pot until the pieces are soft; then stir these and keep up a slow cooking until the moisture has evaporated; especial care is to be taken that the pumpkin shall not scorch; when dry, it is taken out, and, when cold, sifted; and now commences the mystery of pumpkin-pie making; to 2 quarts of the sifted pumpkin, add 3 quarts of milk—⅛ of it being cream—12 eggs, a little salt, a pint of molasses, ½ teaspoonful of ginger, and pounded cinnamon sifted, enough to suit the taste; stir well; have pie-plates lined with paste, with an edge around the top ornamented to suit; stir up from the bottom and fill the plates, and bake, and, when the pie rises up, it is done; they must bake until they crack; all pies with eggs require that the egg only set; if it boils, it wheys.

CHERRY TART.—Have a very shallow round tin tart mould, not more than 1½ inches deep; cover it with a thin layer of paste; then take some fine cherries, cut off their stems with a pair of scissors, so as not to tear the fruit; the beauty of a cherry tart consisting of the fruit being whole, when sent to the table; pack in a single layer of the cherries, strew a good deal of sugar over them, and bake ¾ of an hour in a gentle oven; serve hot or cold.

LEMON PIE.—Take the juice and rind of 1 lemon, 1 cup of sugar, the yolks of 3 eggs, 1 teaspoonful of butter and sufficient milk to fill the plate; bake in a rich paste; beat the whites of the 3 eggs to a stiff froth, with 2 tablespoonfuls of powdered sugar, spread over the pie when a little cool, replace in the oven, and brown slightly; this makes a most delicious pie.

WASHINGTON PIE.—One cup of sugar, ½ cup of butter, ½ cup of sweet milk, 1½ cups of flour, 1 egg, ½ teaspoonful of soda, 1 of cream tartar; lemon flavor; grease 2 round tins, and put in the above; bake until done; then put it on a dinner plate; spread with nice apple sauce, or sauce of any kind; then another layer of cake on top; it is nice without sauce, but sauce improves it.

Cook Book. 37

FRENCH OYSTER PIE.—Pick the oysters well, so that no shells may be found in them; put them in a stew-pan with enough of the liquor to keep them from burning; season with blades of mace, some grated nutmeg, a little lemon-peel, whole pepper and a little finely minced celery; then dredge with flour slightly; add a little fresh butter; let the oysters simmer over the fire, but not boil; just before taking off of the fire, add the yolks of 3 eggs, well beaten, if the pie be small, if large, the yolks of 5 eggs; put your pie crust in your pan, fold a clean cloth or some cotton in the inside, then put your top crust on, and bake light brown, while the oysters are being prepared; when the crust is done, remove from the oven; take off the top crust, and remove the cloth or cotton, and pour in the oysters, then replace the top crust; send to the table hot. Plain Oyster Pie may be made the same way without the seasoning.—*Miss L. R., New York.*

SWEET POTATO PIE.—Boil your potatoes with the skins on, until perfectly done; then skin them and mash well, and rub through a colander; season, and make like pumpkin pie; Irish potatoes made the same way, make a good pie.—*Maggie M. Mc., Philadelphia, Pennsylvania.*

PEACH COBBLER.—Take a bread-pan, line it with the pie crust, then fill it to the top with cut peaches; sprinkle a good deal of sugar over it, a little flour and ½ nutmeg or a little cinnamon, and ½ cup of water; then put on the top crust, and bake until well done; serve with cream. Apple Cobbler can be made the same as peach, by adding a lump of butter the size of a walnut.

BLACKBERRY.—Line the pans with paste, then fill full with well picked berries; cover over the top with white sugar; then put on the top crust; little water must be to the fruit to start it cooking; then it is ready for baking.

CAKES.

DELICATE.—One cup of butter (white), 2 cups of granulated sugar, 4 cups of flour, 1 of sweet milk, 1 teaspoonful of cream tartar in the flour, 1 teaspoonful of soda in a little of the milk and the whites of 8 eggs. The same for gold cake, using the yolks instead of the whites.

WASHINGTON.—Two eggs, two cups of sugar, ½ cup of butter, 1 cup of milk, 3 cups of flour, ½ teaspoonful of soda; beat the butter and sugar together.

38   *The Eclipse*

COCONUT.—Two and two-thirds cups of sugar, 1 cup of butter, 1 cup of sweet milk, 4 cups of flour, the whites of 6 eggs, 1 teaspoonful of soda dissolved in milk, 2 teaspoonfuls of cream tartar in flour; bake in thin cakes and spread frosting between like jelly cake; the whites of 5 eggs will ice it; grate coconut on frosting.

SPICE.—Half a cup of brown sugar, ½ cup of butter, 1 cup of molasses, 2 cups of flour before sifted, 1½ cups of water, 2 eggs, 1 teaspoonful cinnamon, cloves, alspice, 1 small nutmeg, ½ teaspoonful of saleratus dissolved in a little boiling water.

MARBLE.—Use the same for the dark part as the spice cake; white part: Three cups of sifted flour, ½ cup of white sugar, 1 cup of milk, 1 egg, 2 tablespoons of butter, 2 teaspoons of cream tarter and 1 of soda; beat the butter and sugar to a cream, then add the milk and soda, the eggs well beaten, then cream tartar and flour; put it in layers, commencing with the brown.

WHITE.—The whites of 14 eggs well beaten, 1 lb. of white sugar, ¾ lb. of butter, beaten to a cream, and the needful amount of flour; double the quantity when a larger cake is desired; bake very slowly until done; flavor with anything you prefer.

SPONGE —Six eggs, ¾ pint of white sugar; beat yolks and sugar together till light; having beaten the whites well stir them in, flavoring with ¼ teaspoon of vanilla; stir in slowly ¾ pint of flour; bake ½ hour when solid. Pap for same: Half pint of milk, ½ pint of sugar, ¼ teaspoon vanilla and 4 tablespoonfuls of flour; put sugar into milk, let milk come to a boil, then stir in it the flour that has been moistened with water; put in layer as in jelly cake.—*Mrs. J. K. Waltz, New Albany, Ind.*

CUSTARD.—One cup of sugar not quite full, 3 eggs, 1½ cups of flour, 1 teaspoon of baking powder and 1 tablespoonful of water; mix altogether and bake in 2 jelly pans. Custard for the same: One cup of sugar, 2 tablespoonfuls of corn starch, 2 eggs well beaten, 1 pint of milk, pinch of salt; boil milk and add mixture when cooked; add tablespoon of butter and 1 teaspoon of flavoring.—*Mrs. Banister, Terre Haute, Ind.*

PLAIN.—Three eggs beat together, ¾ cup of butter, 1½ cups of brown sugar, 1 cup of sweet milk, one teaspoonful of baking powder, flour enough to make a stiff batter, ½ paper of cinnamon and 1 lb. raisins; bake in square pans.

CREAM.—Two cups of sugar, 1 cup of butter, 1 cup of sweet milk, white of 6 eggs and the yolk of 1, 2 teaspoonfuls of baking powder and 2 cups of flour; after baking spread with jelly; thin with icing; put in the oven and bake a light brown; or use 1 cup of cream sweetened very sweet with white sugar; flavor with vanilla and add 1 cup of dessicated coconut.

BERRY.—One pint of milk, 1 quart of flour, one quart of berries, 1 cup of sugar, 2 eggs, and 3 teaspoonfuls of baking powder.

ROLLED JELLY.—One cup of sugar, 1 tablespoonful of butter, 1½ cups of flour, ¾ cup of milk, 1 egg, 2 teaspoonfuls of baking powder sifted flour; bake in a large sheet; when done spread on the jelly and cut the sheet into strips 3 or 4 inches wide and roll up; if instead of jelly a sauce is used it may be eaten as cream pie.

QUEEN OF HEARTS.—One pound of sifted sugar, 1 lb. of butter, 8 eggs, 1 lb. and 1 quart of flour, 2 oz. of currants and ½ nutmeg grated; cream the butter by mixing with the hands; mix it well with the sugar and spice; then put in half the eggs and beat it 10 minutes; add the remainder of the eggs and beat it 10 minutes longer; stir in the flour lightly and the currants afterwards; bake in hot oven; when done remove from the pans as soon as possible.

STARCH.—Two cups of sugar, 1 cup of corn starch, 1 cup of butter, 2 cups of flour, the whites of 7 eggs and 1 cup of sweet milk; beat the butter and sugar to a stiff cream; mix the milk and starch together, then stir them with the butter and sugar; ½ teaspoonful of cream tartar mixed with the flour and ¼ teaspoonful of soda; stir the whites of the eggs.—*Mrs. Capt. Lee, Omaha.*

QUEEN DROPS.—Take 4 oz. of flour and 2 oz. of currants from the Queen of Hearts receipt; add 2 oz. of candied peel cut small; work the same as the other receipt, and when ready put the measure into a biscuit funnel and lay them out in drops the size of a silver dollar on white paper; bake in a hot oven.

DOUGHNUTS.—Two cups of new milk, ¾ cup of butter, 2 cups of sugar, 2 eggs, 1 cup of warm milk, butter and sugar; stir into a batter, then add the rest; when light knead soft and let rise again; roll out ¾ inch thick; flavor with cinnamon; let stand ½ hour to rise; cut square and boil in hot lard; when brown take them out and sprinkle with white sugar.

MOUNTAIN.—Two cups of white sugar and 1 cup of butter; cream the butter and sugar; 1 cup of sweet milk, 3½ of flour, 3 teaspoons of baking powder mixed with the flour and the whites of 8 eggs; bake as jelly cake; spread the cakes with icing and place together while hot; flavor to suit the taste.

COOKIES.—Needful amount of flour, 3 eggs, 1½ cups of sugar, a little sprinkle of of salt, almost one cup of butter and 1 teaspoonful of soda in a tablespoonful of water; beat the sugar and butter together, then add eggs and flour and soda; bake in a very hot oven.—*Mrs. H. Stacy, Gillman, Ill.*

ROSE.—Make dough like you would for delicate, then take ⅓ of the dough and put in another vessel; take as much alum as can lay on the point of a case knife, and the same amount of cochineal; pour a little boiling water on them and let them steep a short time; strain the fluid through a thin cloth into a vessel containing ⅓ of the dough and stir it well; then put a layer of the white and a layer of the colored alternately in your pan, as you do in marble cake.—*Mrs. William Smock, Indianapolis, Ind.*

ORANGE.—One cup of milk, 1 of melted butter, 3 of sugar, 4½ of flour, 6 eggs, 1 teaspoonful of soda and 2 of cream tartar; mix butter and sugar together to a cream and add 1 egg without beating; bake in jelly pans Jelly for it: One cup of sugar, 2 tablespoons of corn starch, 1 cup of boiling water and the juice of 2 and the rind of 1 orange boiled well together; spread between the cakes when cold.—*Miss Emma Hill.*

SALLY'S COOKIES.—Two cups of sugar, ½ of butter, ½ of lard, 2 eggs, 1 teaspoon of soda, 2 of cream tartar and the needful amount of flour; flavor to suit the taste and bake in a quick oven.

ALMOND.—Beat the yolks and whites of 12 eggs. to a froth, and pound to paste ½ lb. of sweet almonds and 1 oz. of bitter almonds, with a tablespoonful of rose or orange flower water; beat the almonds thoroughly up with the solid froth of the whites of the eggs, then add the yolks and beat in 1 lb. of finely-sifted sugar and the grated rind of 2 lemons; next, ¾ lb. of fine flour and gradually 1 lb. of clarified butter, warm, but not hot; beat the batter very much till perfectly well mixed; then pour into a buttered mould which will leave space for the cake to rise; bake it for 2 hours; but when half done put a buttered paper over the top to prevent the cake from being scorched.—*F. C. B., Chicago.*

Cook Book. 41

MACAROONS.—Time, 15 to 20 minutes; blanch 8 oz. of fine almonds and pound in a mortar to a smooth paste, with 2 teaspoonfuls of rose or orange flower water; whisk up the whites of 8 eggs to a solid froth and add to it 1 lb. of finely-sifted sugar, then beat in by degrees the almond paste till thoroughly mixed ! have ready confectioner's wafer paper and drop the mixture upon it in small rounds; bake in a moderate oven till lightly colored.

CHOCOLATE.—One lb. of flour, 1 lb. of sugar, 1 lb. of butter, 8 eggs, 2 tablespoonfuls of vinegar from sweet pickles, a pinch of salt and chocolate glazing; mix the above ingredients well together with a wooden spoon, putting the butter (melted before the fire) in last; spread a baking sheet with butter, put over it the mixture ½ inch thick and bake it; cut the cake into oblong pieces and glaze thickly with chocolate.

NUT.—One cup of butter, 2 of sugar, 5 eggs, ½ teaspoonful of soda dissolved in 1 cup of sweet milk, 1 of cream tartar, 1 pint of hickory-nut meats, 1 lb. of raisins and 1 of flour; 3 tablespoonfuls of infallible yeast powder is better than the soda and cream tartar.

SUGARED ALMONDS.—Make a syrup of 1 pint of water to a pound of sugar, and when boiling stir in blanched Jordan almonds for 10 minutes; take them out and dry and reduce the syrup one half; then dip the almonds in again for a minute and with the thick syrup adhering to them dry them on an inverted sieve in a warm place and store in a tin box.

ORNAMENTAL FROSTING.—Whites of eggs, sugar and coloring; for this purpose, have syringes of different sizes, draw any one you may choose full of the icing and work it in any designs you may fancy; wheels, Grecian borders or flowers look well, or borders of beading; the cake must first be covered with a plain frosting, which may be white or colored pink, with extract of cochineal, blue with a little indigo, or brown with a little chocolate finely grated, green with a little spinach juice.

FRUIT CAKE.—Three eggs beat well together, ¾ cup of butter, 1½ cups of brown sugar, 1 cup of sweet milk, 1 cup of strong coffee prepared as for table, 1½ teaspoonfuls baking powder, flour enough to make a stiff batter, 1 lb. of raisins, 1 lb. currants, 2 oz. of orange prepared, same of lemon, spice to suit the taste and a sprinkle of mace and citron; bake in slow oven until thoroughly done.—*S. B., New Albany.*

ICE CREAM.—Two cups of sugar, 1 cup butter, $3\frac{1}{2}$ flour, 1 sweet milk, whites of 8 eggs and 2 tablespoonfuls baking powder. Icing for the above: Whites of 3 eggs beaten to a froth, mix 2 cups of powdered sugar with water enough to make it moist; boil to a thick syrup and pour over the eggs; stir mixture until nearly cold, then flavor.—*Mrs. Banister.*

PAP FOR CAKE.—Usual float thickened with flour, lemon icing, juice of 1 lemon, tablespoonful of water, 1 cup or more of powdered sugar.

GOLD AND SILVER.—One cup of butter, 2 of sugar, 1 cup sweet milk, whites of 8 eggs, if your measuring cup be small, 9 if large; 4 full cups of flour, 2 teaspoonfuls of baking powder; beat till very light and flavor to suit the taste. Gold cake exactly the same, excepting the yolks instead of the whites; if a large cake is desired double the quantity.—*Mrs. W. S.*

GINGER SNAPS.—One cup of lard, 1 of sugar, 2 of molasses, 1 teaspoonful of soda dissolved in a cup of water, 3 teaspoonfuls of ginger; mix very stiff.

SPONGE.—Twelve eggs beaten separately, then mixed and beaten till very light; add a heaping pint of white sugar, a teaspoonful of vanilla; slowly stir in $1\frac{1}{2}$ pints of flour; bake over $\frac{1}{2}$ hour.

POUND.—Twelve eggs beaten separately, 1 quart of white sugar beaten well with yolks, not quite 1 lb. of butter; beat well; teaspoonful of vanilla; slowly stir in a little over a quart of flour; bake about $1\frac{1}{2}$ hours.—*Miss Emma Hill.*

CHOCOLATE (excellent).—One good cup of butter, 2 cups of sugar, beat till thin, add the yolks of 5 eggs, next the whites of 3 eggs well beaten, scant cup of milk; finally stir in not quite 4 cups of flour, containing 2 teaspoonfuls of baking powder, or $\frac{1}{2}$ teaspoonful of soda and 1 of cream tartar. Frosting for the cake: The whites of 2 eggs, $1\frac{1}{2}$ cups of powdered sugar, 2 teaspoonfuls of vanilla, 6 tablespoonfuls of grated chocolate; to be baked in a dripping pan in a thin loaf and frosted while hot; do not take out of pan until desired for consumption.

FEATHER (cheap and good).—One tablespoon butter, 1 cup sugar, 1 egg, 1 cup milk, 1 teaspoon cream tartar, $\frac{1}{2}$ teaspoon soda, 2 cups flour, nutmeg.

Cook Book. 43

BOSTON CREAM.—Take 1 pint of water, ¼ lb. of butter, ¾ lb. flour; put the butter in the water when boiling and stir in the flour, taking care that it is free from lumps; then pour into a dish to cool; when cool beat in 10 eggs, 1 at a time; butter tin sheets and drop it on in small thick rounds; bake in a quick oven. Cream for the above: Take 1 quart of milk, ¼ lb. of flour; wet the flour with part of the milk and put the rest over the fire to boil; then stir in the flour and allow it to boil 1 minute; beat 4 eggs with ½ lb. of powdered sugar and stir in while hot; add salt and extract lemon to the taste; when the cakes have become cold, open them at one side and put in them the cream.—*Miss Longnecker, Columbus, Ohio.*

FRUIT.—Take ½ cup of molasses, 6 cups of flour, 3 cups of sugar, 2 cups of butter, 1 cup of milk, 5 eggs, 2 nutmegs, 2 teaspoonfuls cloves powdered, 2 teaspoonfuls ground alspice, 2 teaspoonfuls ground cinnamon, about ¼ oz. of mace, 1 wine-glass of vinegar of spiced pickles, 2 lbs. of currants, 2 lbs. of raisins, 1 teaspoonful soda; bake carefully in a well-heated oven.

HARD TIMES.—Take 1 cup of molasses and 1 cup of dried apples and simmer together; 1 cup of sugar, ½ cup of milk, 2½ cups of flour, 1 egg and 1 teaspoonful of baking powder.

COFFEE.—This very much resembles black cake and is very nice indeed; 2 cups of sugar, 1 of butter, 1 of coffee, 1 tablespoonful of cinnamon, 1 of cloves, 1 of soda, 1 nutmeg, 1 lb. of stoned raisins; you can use either sugar or molasses; prepare the coffee as for the table, no eggs, 3½ cups of flour; let it remain in the pan in which it is baked to cool.—*Mrs. M. G. Miller, Columbus, Ohio.*

WHITE POUND.—One pound of pulverized sugar, 1 lb. flour, ¾ lb. of butter, with salt washed out, ⅓ teaspoonful of saleratus; lemon or vanilla flavoring.—*Mrs. Miller.*

COOKIES, OR JUMBLES.—Two cups sugar, 1 cup butter, 4 eggs, flour enough to roll stiff; 2 tablespoons lard substitute butter very nicely and tastes as well.

PORK.—One lb. of pork chopped fine, ½ cup of boiling water poured over 3 cups of sugar, 2 of milk and 2 lbs. of raisins or currants.

COCOANUT DROPS.—One lb. of cocoanut, 1 lb sugar, 4 eggs and 4 tablespoonfuls of flour.

44   *The Eclipse*

BREAD (excellent).—Two cups raised dough, 2 cups sugar, 1 cup butter creamed, 3 eggs, 2 teaspoons yeast powder, 2 tablespoonfuls milk, ¼ lb. currants, nutmegs, cloves and cinnamon to taste; stir until all are well mixed; put in the beaten eggs, and, lastly, fruit well floured; let rise 20 minutes in buttered pans.— *Alice Shade, Columbus, Ohio.*

FRUIT CUP.—One cup of sweet butter and 3 of nice sugar worked to a cream, 5 well-beaten eggs, the yolks and afterward the whites, ½ a nutmeg, ½ dozen cloves and a teaspoonful of ground cinnamon; pulverize a teaspoonful of soda, mix it in 5 cups of sifted flour and stir the flour in the cake; flour 1 lb. of washed currants and mix them in, and afterward 1 lb. of seeded raisins cut once and rubbed in flour; stir it well, and just before baking add a cup of sour cream; do not beat it much after the cream is in, but thoroughly mix and bake immediately; it will take 1 hour to bake; frost while a little warm; it will keep fresh some time; do not cut it the day it is baked; this is an old but excellent receipt.

DELICATE CUP.—One cup of butter, 3 of loaf sugar pulverized, the whites of 10 eggs, 5 cups of flour in which 2 teaspoonfuls of cream of tartar have been mixed and sifted; the flour must always be sifted before measuring and then again after the tartar is in; and, lastly, a cup of sweet cream, with a teaspoonful of soda dissolved in it and strained; this can be varied by mixing through it a few currants.

RICH SODA.—One lb. of pulverized loaf-sugar mixed with ¾ lb. of sweet butter, the beaten whites of fourteen eggs and 2 teaspoonfuls of cream of tartar, sifted with 1 lb. of flour; and, lastly, a teaspoonful of soda dissolved in ½ teacupful of sweet milk, and strained; bake immediately.

DESSERTS.

CHARLOTTE RUSSE OF APPLES AND APRICOTS.—Line a plain mould with Savoy biscuits dipped in clarified butter, exactly placed upright, to join so that the contents of the Charlotte do not escape; cut off the ends to make it stand firm; fill the mould with fresh apple jelly, or marmalade, with a spoonful of apricot jam, or raspberry jelly in the centre; cover the mould with buttered biscuits closely as at the sides; put a dish over it, and bake for half an hour in a quick oven; then turn over out of the mould, and serve hot.

FLOATING ISLAND.—One quart of milk, put in a small bucket, and set in a pot of warm water, to prevent the milk from scorching; let the milk come to a boil, then add 3 well-beaten eggs; sweeten and flavor to taste; when the eggs thicken a little, remove and let cool; when ready for the table, beat the whites of 3 or 4 eggs to a froth; soften a little red jelly, and beat in with the froth; put on top of the custard.

CHARLOTTE RUSSE.—Take 1 quart of rich milk and make a boiled custard, sweeten to the taste and flavor with vanilla or lemon; boil 1 oz. of isinglass in a little water until dissolved, then stir the isinglass in the custard; when the custard becomes cool, stir in 1 pint of whipped cream, and when it begins to stiffen pour it into your dish lined with sponge cake; the cream may be very cold or it will not foam when you beat it.—*Mrs. H. J. Hawke.*

ORANGE CUSTARD.—Pour over 6 oz. of sugar in a pan, the juice of 6 oranges, and let it simmer to a syrup; then pour it out to cool; beat up very well the yolks of 6 eggs, and mix with a pint of good cream; set them over a slow fire, and stir continually till the custard thickens and begins to simmer; mix the syrup gradually, and stir a few minutes longer; then turn out, and stir till cold, when it can be transferred to the custard-dish or cups.

BLANCMANGE.—Time, 15 minutes; 1 oz. of isinglass or gelatine, 2 oz. of blanched or pounded almonds, 1 oz. of bitter ones, 1½ pint of milk, 1 pint of cream, 1 lemon, a spoonful of rosewater, and 2 oz loaf sugar; put into a delicately-clean stew-pan the isinglass, or gelatine, the sweet and bitter almonds, blanched or pounded, the new milk and cream, the lemon-juice, and the peel grated, with loaf sugar to taste; set the stew-pan over a clear fire, and stir it till nearly cool before putting it into the mould; this quantity will fill a quart mould, but if you wish to make it in a smaller shape, you must not put more than a pint of milk and ½ of cream; color the top ornament with cochineal, and let it get cold before you add the rest of the blancmange.

PINEAPPLE ICE CREAM.—To ½ lb. of preserved pineapple pounded with sugar, add sugar and lemon juice to palate, 1 pint of cream, and a little new milk; mix; freeze; 1 quart; or, take a pineapple weighing about ½ lb., cut it in pieces, bruise it in a mortar; add ½ lb. of sugar, the juice of 1 lemon; rub them well together in the mortar; pass through a hair sieve; freeze; a few slices of preserved pineapple may be added when frozen; 1 quart.

GERMAN PUFFS —One pint of milk, 5 eggs, 2 oz. butter, 8 tablespoonfuls of flour, 2 teaspoonfuls of sugar, 1 heaping teaspoonful corn starch; bake in cups and serve with sauce or sweetened and flavored cream.

ARROW ROOT BLANCMANGE.—Infuse 2 oz. of arrow root in cold water for 20 minutes; then pour off the water, and blend the arrow. root with a tablespoonful of cream or orange-flower water; boil a quart of new milk with 4 oz. of sugar, half a lemon-peel, a stick of cinnamon, and a teaspoonful of ratafia or pudding flavor; pour the milk over the arrow root, stirring it continually till cool; then pour into a mould, and leave it to set.

LEMON ICE CREAM.—Take 1 pint of cream, $\frac{1}{2}$ teaspoonful extract of lemon, or take the juice of 2 lemons, $\frac{1}{2}$ lb. sugar; mix; freeze; 1 quart.

STRAWBERRY ICE CREAM.—Pick some strawberries (the scarlet are considered the best) into a basin or pan; add sugar in powder, with a quantity of strawberry jam equal to the fruit, the juice or a lemon or two, according to palate, a small quantity of new milk, and a pint of fresh cream; mix, and add a little color; freeze; 1 quart; or, when fresh strawberries cannot be procured, take 1 lb. of strawberry jam, the juice of 1 or 2 lemons, 1 pint or cream, and a little milk; color; freeze; 1 quart.

LEMON CUSTARD.—Beat the yolks of 8 eggs $\frac{1}{2}$ hour to froth, and strain them; pour over them a pint of boiling water and the outer rind of 2 lemons, grated; make the juice of the 2 lemons into a syrup, with 3 oz. of sugar, and stir into the custard; then set it over the fire, adding a glass and a half of spiced vinegar, and stir till it thickens; pour it out, and stir till cold; then serve in cups.

ITALIAN ICE CREAM.—Rasp 2 lemons on some sugar, compress the juice from the lemons, or use $\frac{1}{2}$ teaspoonful extract of lemon, to which add 1 pint of cream, $\frac{1}{2}$ lb. of sugar; freeze; 1 quart.

CHARLOTTE RUSSE, (excellent).—Take 1 quart of cream, beat to a froth, with a dozen eggs, well-beaten; sweeten and flavor; put $\frac{1}{2}$ box of geletine in the milk, sufficient to moisten it, and set it where it will warm gradually; stir often; when dissolved, add the prepared cream; line a dish with sponge cake, sliced, or lady fingers; pour the cream into it; set in a cool place.—*Mrs. Cobb, Chicago.*

Cook Book. 47

GROUND RICE BLANCMANGE.—Mix gradually 4 oz. of fine ground rice with a pint and a half of good new milk; if a part of this be cream, it greatly improves the blancmange; to this add 3 oz. of powdered sugar, and a teaspoonful of ratafia or pudding-flavor; stir it over the fire, continually beating it to prevent it running into lumps, and simmer it for 35 minutes; then pour it into a mould dipped into cold water, and leave it in a cool place to set.

STRAWBERRY BLANCMANGE.—One quart of ripe strawberries, 2 oz. of isinglass, ½ lb. loaf sugar, juice of 1 lemon, 1¼ pints of cream, 1 pint of milk; crush a quart of strawberries with a silver or wooden spoon, and strew over them ¼ lb. of powdered sugar, let them stand for several hours, and then press them through a hair sieve reversed; dissolve 2 oz. of isinglass in a pint of boiling milk and the remaining ¼ lb. of sugar, then strain it through muslin, and stir it into the cream, and continue to stir it until nearly cold; then pour it gradually to the strawberries, whisking it quickly together; add the lemon juice, a few drops at a time, to prevent its curdling, and then put it into an oiled mould in a cold place, to set for 12 or 14 hours.

RASPBERRY OR CURRANT CUSTARD.—Make a rich syrup of a pint of raspberry or currant juice, poured over 8 oz. of loaf sugar; skim it, and stir gradually into it over a very slow fire the well-beaten yolks of 6 eggs, and continue to stir for 5 or 6 minutes; then pour it out, and as it cools stir in by degrees ½ pint of cream and a tablespoonful of lemon juice.

IRISH MOSS.—Take a handful of the moss, soak an hour, then pick and wash through 3 or 4 waters; have ready a quart of boiling milk, sweeten and flavor to suit the taste; put in the moss and let it cook, stirring most of the time while it is dissolving; when of the consistency of starch strain into mould and let cool; eat with cream and sugar.—*Mrs. Captain W. H. Bisbee, Fort Bridger, Wyoming.*

SNOW BALLS.—Pare 5 large baking apples, taking out the cores with a scoop; fill the holes with orange, quince or any other kind of marmalade; then make a little hot paste and roll your apples in it; make your crust of equal thickness, put them in a pan and bake them in a moderate oven; make icing as for cake and ice them over; set them a good distance before the fire; do not let them brown; serve with sauce.—*Mrs. James Taylor, Sheffield, England.*

SNOW CREAM.—Make a rich custard, put it in the bottom of your glass dish, then take the whites of 8 eggs, beat with rose water and a spoonful of treble refined sugar; beat it till it is a strong froth; put some milk and water into a broad stew-pan and when it boils take the froth off the eggs, lay it on the milk and water and let it boil once up; take it off carefully and lay it on your custard; it is a pretty dish for supper.—*Mrs. Taylor.*

ANGLES FOOD.—Slice some oranges, and lay in alternate layers, with grated cocoanut; sweeten with loaf sugar.—*Mrs. Raby, Tennessee.*

CANDIES.

ALMOND NAGAT.—Two lbs. of sweet almonds, 1 lb. of sugar, 1 lb. of water. Blanch the almonds and cut them in slices, dry them at the mouth of a cool oven, and if slightly browned, the better; powder the sugar and put into a stew-pan with the water, place it on the fire to melt, stirring it with a spatula until it becomes a fine brown, then mix in the almonds and let them be well covered with the sugar; pour it out on a greased plate. Any other nut may be used in making Nagat.

BUTTER SCOTCH.—Half pint of molasses, 2 ounces of butter, 1 pound of sugar, boil altogether over a clear fire! when you think it is done, take a little out, drop it on the plate, if it hardens it is enough; grease a tin and pour it out on your tin; cut it in pieces before it is too hard.

TAFFY.—One quart of white sugar, 1 pint of water, ¼ pint of vinegar, butter the size of large walnut. Be careful not to stir while cooking if you want it white.—*Eva Lattimer.*

CHOCOLATE CAROMELS.—Three lbs. white sugar, ¼ lb. fresh butter, 1 teaspoon of pure cream tartar, 1 teaspoon of vanilla; boil like ice cream candy; only boil to a hard ball; when it comes to a hard ball, put in your butter and chocolate, then pour on a marble slab and cut with a caromel cutter; always dissolve your butter and chocolate before putting it in the candy, just before taking off all your vanilla.—*J. Dixon, Columbus, O.*

MAPLE WAX.—Two lbs. maple sugar, 1 lb. brown sugar, ½ gallon water, lemon oil; boil as ice cream candy, only let it come to a hard ball; when done, add a few drops of lemon oil, then pour into pans well greased with butter; when cold, cut in squares with a knife.—*J. Dixon.*

Cook Book. 49

COCOANUT CREAM.—Three lbs. white sugar, 1 grated cocoanut, ½ gallon water, ¼ teaspoon of pure cream tartar; boil until it comes to a soft ball, then set off until cold, then put in the cocoanut, add a few drops of lemon oil, then with a paddle rub the candy on the sides of the kettle until it is grained, then stir the cocoanut and candy thoroughly for 5 or 10 minutes, then with a spoon drop it in small cakes on a greased tin.—*J. Dixon.*

ICE CREAM CANDY.—Five lbs. white sugar, ½ teaspoonful of pure cream tartar, 1 gallon water, 1 tablespoon of vanilla; to be boiled in a copper kettle; to tell when it is done, take a stick and wet it, and put it in the candy and get a little of the candy on it and then cool it in the water, and when it will crack and break in your hand, it is done; then drop a lump of fresh butter in it, stir a moment, then pour on a marble slab well greased with butter or lard; when cool enough to handle, put on an iron hook and flavor with vanilla; pull until white; always keep a steamer on the kettle while cooking.—*J. Dixon.*
Soft ball means, when it pulls soft; hard ball means, when it is hard and cracks,

CHOCOLATE CREAM.—Three lbs. white sugar, ½ gallon water, ½ teaspoon of pure cream tartar, ¼ lb chocolate, 6 oz. butter with the salt washed out; put your sugar, water and cream tartar into a copper kettle, cook until it comes to a hard ball, then set off; put your chocolate and butter into a small stirring pan and place on stove until the chocolate is thoroughly dissolved, then set it off; if your candy is cool, add a tablespoonful of vanilla, then commence stirring it with a paddle against the sides of the kettle until it is grained and creamy, then pour it in a greased pan, and then warm up your chocolate and pour over the cream; when cold, cut in slices.—*J. Dixon.*

CHOCOLATE CREAM DROPS.—Four lbs. white sugar, ½ gallon water, ½ teaspoon of pure cream tartar; boil in copper kettle until it comes to a hard ball, then set it off until cold, then grain it with a paddle by rubbing the candy with the paddle on the side of the kettle; keep stirring until it is creamy white and stiff, then take 6 oz. fresh butter, ¼ lb. chocolate, and put in a small stirring pan, place on the fire and stir until the chocolate is thoroughly dissolved, then set off; if by this time the cream is hard enough, take and roll it up in little balls, and when you have done this, warm up the chocolate and with a fork dip the cream balls in it, and then place in a greasy tin until the chocolate becomes hard.—*J. Dixon.*

MACCARONIES.—One and one-half pounds almonds, or any other kind of nuts, 18 whites of eggs, 3 lbs. white sugar, lemon oil; put the almonds in a mortar and pound with a pestle until they are very fine, then add your sugar, then the eggs—three at a time—stir them well until all the eggs are used; in making good maccaronies, it depends upon the stirring of your eggs whether your maccaronies are good or not; the more you stir your eggs, the better your maccaronies will be; when the eggs are all used, drop on brown paper, bake in quick oven.

CAROMELS.—Two cups of brown sugar, one cup of molasses, a piece of butter the size of an egg; three tablespoonsful of flour; boil these together for 25 minutes, then add ½ lb. of grated chocolate dissolved in one cup of sweet milk; let it boil until it will harden when dropped into water, stirring constantly; take it from the fire and add one teaspoonful of vanilla, pour it in buttered plates to cool; just before it is hard, make it into small squares.— *M. Hill, Chicago, Ill.*

MAPLE TAFFY.—Three lbs. of maple sugar, 1 lb. brown sugar, ¼ lb. butter, ½ gallon water, lemon oil; boil as you do ice cream candy; pour on marble slab; when cool, put on hook, then flavor; put in the butter when done boiling.—*J. Dixon.*

MISCELLANEOUS.

TOMATO PRESERVES.—Take the round yellow variety as soon as ripe, scald and peel; then to 7 lbs. of tomatoes add 7 lbs. of white sugar and let them stand over night; take the tomatoes out of the sugar and boil the syrup, removing the scum; put in the tomatoes and boil gently 15 or 20 minutes; remove the fruit again and boil until the syrup thickens; on cooling, put the fruit into the jars and pour the syrup over it, adding a few slices of lemon to each jar, and you will have something to suit the taste of the most fastidious.

TOMATO CASUP.—Take ripe tomatoes and scald them just sufficient to allow you to take off the skin; then let them stand for a day, covered with salt; strain them thoroughly to remove the seed; then to every quart, 2 oz. of cloves, 2 of black pepper, 2 nutmegs and a very little cayenne pepper, with a little salt; boil the liquor for ½ hour and then let it cool and settle; add a pint of the best cider vinegar, after which bottle it, corking and sealing it tightly; keep it always in a cool place.

Cook Book. 51

ANOTHER WAY.—Take 1 bushel of tomatoes and boil them until they are soft; squeeze them through a fine wire sieve and add ⅓ gallon of vinegar, 1½ pints of salt, 2 oz. of cloves, ¼ lb. of allspice, 2 oz. cayenne pepper, 3 teaspoonfuls of black pepper, 5 heads of garlic, skinned and separated; mix together and boil about 3 hours, or until reduced to about one-half; then bottle, without straining.

ARROWROOT.—Not quite a tablespoonful of arrowroot powder is to be mixed with a little cold water, and when done a pint of boiling water added; it should then be sweetened to taste and put on the fire to boil for 5 minutes, stirring well the whole time; if spiced vinegar is permitted it should be put to it after the arrowroot is poured into the basin; the same quantity of arrowroot is a proper one when it is prepared with milk instead of water.

OATMEAL GRUEL.—A dessertspoonful of meal must be mixed smoothly with 2 of cold water, a pint of boiling water poured on and the whole boiled on the fire for 10 minutes, stirring well for the time; sugar or pepper and salt being added, as may be agreeable to or proper for the sick person.

GROUND RICE MILK.—A tablespoonful of ground rice, 1½ pints of milk and ½ oz. of candied lemon peel; mix the rice very smoothly with the milk, then add the lemon peel cut into very small pieces; boil for ½ hour and strain as soon as off the fire; this is an excellent, nutritious beverage for the sick when strict abstinence is not required, and for early convalescence.

SIMPLE BREAD PANADA.—Put a moderate quantity of grated or soft stale bread into enough boiling water to form a moderately thick pulp; cover it up and leave it to soak for an hour; then beat it up with 2 or 3 tablespoonfuls of milk and fine sugar to sweeten; boil the whole for 10 minutes; this preparation is occasionally acceptable to the invalid, when milk dietary alone is rejected.

TOAST WATER.—This simple beverage is seldom well prepared; let the water with which it is made, have been boiled and become cold; toast thoroughly of a fine deep brown, but not black, half a slice of stale quarter loaf; put it into a jug, and pour a quart of the water over it; let it stand 2 hours, and decant the water from the bread; a small piece of either orange or lemon-peel, added with the bread, is an improvement to toast water.

CARRAGEEN MOSS.—One oz. of it, boiled in 1½ pints of water, is sufficient to form a semi-transparent, moderately consistent, nearly tasteless jelly, which, when sweetened and acidulated, or when mixed with milk, forms an excellent diet for invalids, who require to have their strength supported; the gelatine, now so commonly used, is a very palatable preparation, combined with either water or milk, and may be taken dissolved in tea, coffee or broth, without impairing the flavor of one or the other.

LINSEED TEA.—One oz. of linseed, not bruised, 2 drachms of liquorice root, bruised; pour over 1 pint of boiling water; place the jug—covered jugs with perforated spouts should always be used for drinks for sick people—near the fire for 3 or 4 hours, then strain off; when linseed tea is ordered to be continued, it should be made fresh every day.

MILK AND SODA WATER.—Heat, nearly to boiling, a teacupful of milk; dissolve in it a teaspoonful of fine sugar, put it into a large tumbler, and pour over it ¾ of a bottle of soda water; this is an excellent mode of taking milk when the stomach is charged with acid, and consequently feels oppressed by milk alone.

RICE AND GRAVY.—Let the rich gravy from a leg of roasted mutton, or sirloin of beef, stand till the fat forms a cake on the surface, remove it, and heat the gravy with as much well-boiled rice as will make it thick; a teacupful of this is very strengthening in the early convalescence of delicate children.

A SUBSTITUTE FOR PRESERVES.—A lady writer in an exchange communicates the following bit of information obtained where she "took tea last:" A dish of what I took to be preserves was passed to me, which, upon tasting, I was surprised to learn it contained no fruit.—The ease with which it was prepared, and the trifling cost of its materials, are not its chief recommendation, for unless my tasting apparatus deceived me, as it is not usually wont to do, it is emphatically a tip-top substitute for apple-sauce, apple-butter, tomato preserves and all that sort of thing. Its preparation is as follows: Moderately boil a pint of molasses from 5 to 20 minutes, according to its consistency, then add 3 eggs thoroughly beaten, hastily stirring them in, and continue to boil a few minutes longer, when season with a nutmeg or lemon.

BEEF TEA.—Take ¼ lb. of lean beef, 1½ pints of water, salt to taste; when it begins to boil, add a little mace; continue the boiling for a short time, when it will be ready.

Cook Book. 53

To Cook Vegetables.—A German professor says, that if one portion of a vegetable be boiled in pure distilled or rain water, and another in water in which a little salt has been added, a decided difference is perceptible in the tenderness of the two. Vegetables boiled in pure water are vastly inferior in flavor. This inferiority may go so far, in the case of onions, that they are almost entirely destitute of either taste or odor; though, when cooked in salt water, in addition to the pleasant salt taste, is a peculiar sweetness and a strong aroma. They also contain more soluble matter than when cooked in pure water. Water which contains one-twentieth of its weight in salt, is far better for cooking vegetables than pure water, because the salt hinders the solution and evaporation of the soluble and flavoring principles of the vegetables.

Chicken Broth.—Take one-half of a carefully-dressed chicken, and pour on it 1 quart of cold water; add a little salt and a teaspoonful of rice; boil very slowly for 2 hours in a tightly-covered vessel; skim occasionally, and season very little.

An Antidote for Tobacco.—Gentian root coarsely ground, chewed well and the saliva swallowed, will cure the appetite for tobacco, if its use is persisted in for a few weeks; take as much of it after each meal, or oftener, as amounts to a common quid of "fine cut" or "cavendish."

C. G. ZIEGFELD & SON'S STAR BAKERY, at 346 East Friend Street, and every Market Day at Stand No. 31, north of Rich St.

J. G. MAIER & Son, Dealers in Dry Goods and Notions, Trimmings, Hosiery, Gloves, &c., 149 East Friend St., Columbus, O.

A. McADOW, Dealer in China, Glass and Queensware, Oil, Fluid and Gasoline Lamps, &c., No. 67 East Friend Street, Columbus.

SEWERAGE & DRAINAGE.— If you want a good job of Sewer, Paving or Guttering done, call on Wentz & Co., 153 E. Fulton St.

CITIZENS' SAVINGS BANK, 40 North High Street, between Gay and Broad, Columbus, O.

JOHN SMITH, Boot and Shoe Maker, No. 102½ South Fourth Street. Repairing done to order on short notice.

A. N. HILL & CO., Clothing and Furnishing Goods House, No. 45 South High St., old Post Office Arcade, Columbus, O.

GENERAL FIRE INSURANCE AGENCY, both Mutual and Stock Plan. S. K. Mann, 26 North High St., Columbus, O.

GO to the Largest and Cheapest Hat, Cap, Straw Goods and Millinery House in the city, J. S. Koch & Son, 174 S. High St.

SARGENT & HANIVAN, Dealers in Butter, Eggs and Produce, No. 170 South Fourth Street, Columbus, Ohio.